SPORTS BEHIND THE IRON CURTAIN

BE BACK

BEHIND THE SCENES OF SPORTS

SPORTS BEHIND THE IRON CURTAIN

is the first in a new series of books that tell the
inside story of the world's major spectator
sports. Written by experts and heavily
illustrated, the series takes a unique look behind
the headlines, the stars and the spectacle at
what makes top international sport tick.

To be published shortly:
GYMNASTICS
SOCCER

In preparation:
BOXING
GOLF
MOTOR RACING
HORSE RACING AND EQUESTRIAN SPORTS

Book designed by Stonecastle Graphics

BEHIND THE SCENES OF SPORTS

SPORTS BEHIND THE IRON CURTAIN

SIMON FREEMAN
AND ROGER BOYES

PROTEUS

London and New York

PROTEUS BOOKS is an imprint of
The Proteus Publishing Group

United Kingdom
PROTEUS (PUBLISHING) LIMITED
Bremar House,
Sale Place,
London, W2 1PT

United States
PROTEUS PUBLISHING COMPANY
distributed by:
LIPPINCOTT & CROWELL PUBLISHERS, INC.
521 Fifth Avenue,
New York, NY 10017

ISBN 0 906071 35 6

Typeset in England by
Flowery Typesetting Ltd.,
and printed and bound
in Singapore by
Toppan Printing Co. (S) Pte. Ltd.

Our thanks are due to many academics, journalists, sportsmen and officials. But we are particularly grateful to the following: Bradford University Russian lecturer James Riordan, whose work is both extensive and authoritative; to Dr. David Childs, one of the West's leading experts on East Germany; to Ron Pickering, coach and BBC commentator; to journalists Ian Wooldridge (*Daily Mail,* London), Hans Voskamp (*Algemeen Dagblad,* Rotterdam), Christopher Brasher (*Observer,* London), John Rodda (*Guardian,* London) and Neil Allen (*Evening Standard,* London). Many thanks, too, to members of the *Der Spiegel* staff and to Reuters journalist Derek Parr for his work in East Berlin. Thanks also to colleagues and friends David Dodwell (*Financial Times,* London) and David Smith (ITN, London) for their advice and encouragement. We are indebted to Chelsea College's Professor Arnold Beckett for his help on drugs and to four officials of the Soviet Sports and Culture Ministry. But they, unfortunately, will have to stay anonymous. Above all we must pay tribute to the many ordinary East European citizens, both sportsmen and fans, who talked to us, often at great personal risk.

The following publications have proved especially valuable: *Sport in Soviety Society,* James Riordan, Cambridge University Press, 1977; *War Without Weapons,* Philip Goodhart and Christopher Chataway, W. H. Allen, 1968; *Sport und Politik in Osteuropa,* Wolf Oscilies, Cologne, 1970; *Blood and Guts, Violence in Sport,* Don Ayteo, Paddington Press, 1979; *Wirklichkeit der Modernen Olympischen Spiele,* Hans Lenk, Stuggart, 1964; *Wettkampf der Nationen, Die Bilanz der Olympischen Spiele,* Bono Harenberg, Dusseldorf, 1968; *Verschenkter Lorbeer, Deutsche Sportler zwischen Ost und West,* Willi Knecht Knecht, Cologne, 1969.

Contents

Introduction

At times the Communist world seems to be ruled by flattering statistics. Newspapers announce the shattering of industrial production targets while schools, farms and factories break records with suspicious regularity. Officially, there is no bad news behind the Iron Curtain. All this tends to devalue even the genuine achievements of the Soviet Union and its allies.

There is, however, one important area where the figures cannot be faked – sport. Just two sets of statistics will show how astounding Communist sporting success has been over the past two decades. Fact one: in 1952, when the Soviet bloc first entered the Olympics, they won 29 per cent of the medals. In Montreal in 1976 they carried off 57 per cent of the medals. Fact two: East Germany, with a population of only 17 million, won more medals in Montreal than the United States, Canada, the United Kingdom and France combined.

How did the Iron Curtain countries manage this staggering improvement? What is the secret of the Communist medal winning machine? There is no question that the system which has brought this success is regarded as sensitive, in some areas as actually secret, by the Communist authorities. For example, in our researches of East German, Russian and other Communist records it was clear that references to the special training schools for young athletes, the use of drugs and sponsorship of sport by the security forces had been excised.

But beneath the mountains of propaganda we have found grains of truth. And with the help of defectors, of experts on drugs, of Sovietologists and even of occasionally indiscreet Communist sports officials, we have managed to build up a picture of how the sports system really functions behind the Iron Curtain.

The book is, we believe, one of the first to examine what actually happens in the training schools of East Germany, the Soviet Union and Cuba. It is one of the first, too, to look at the financing of Communist sport and the mysterious ties between the KGB security service and the successful Dynamo sports club.

It is worth remembering when Russian or East German athletes flash past the winning post at the Moscow Olympics in 1980 that there is a darker side to Communist sport. What happens to the failures – to top-class athletes who suddenly lose form or who are dishonoured? Men like Boris Onischenko, the Soviet fencer, who was caught cheating at the Montreal Games? And what happens to the non-conformists, the Olga Korbuts, who are constantly under pressure to adapt their sporting styles to the acceptable Soviet pattern? Winning is not the only thing that matters in Communist sport; conforming is an equally strong element.

SPORT BEHIND THE IRON CURTAIN looks at both the successes and failures. And we try too to see if there are any alternatives to the rigid win-or-else philosophy that dominates sport in the Communist world. Both China and Cuba, we believe, offer hope that the role of sport under Communsim may change in the coming years. Cuba, for example, proves that it is not necessary to spend millions of roubles, marks or dollars to produce competent – and apparently happy – sportsmen. And China, which once claimed that friendship had to come before competition, is now challenging the traditional view that sport is simply a tool for winning international prestige.

In pointing out the areas where Communist sport and politics become intertwined, we have run the risk of seeming anti-sport. We are not. We are not even anti-politics. But we do believe that the relationship between sport and politics needs to be clarified soon if international sports, and especially the great amateur festivals like the Olympics, are to survive.

International sport can, and does, foster friendship between nations. Recent soccer matches between England and West Germany – notably the World Cup Final at Wembley, London in 1966 – have been sporting epics; notable for their good humor as much as a supreme level of play. We could have pointed to the role of sport in developing a much-needed interest in the Third World. The sight of Africans or Asians with tongue-twisting names competing against our own men and women must mean that we become more concerned about the problems of those distant countries. We could have argued that it is infinitely better for Americans and Rus

sians to fight it out with running shoes and boxing gloves rather than with nuclear missiles and cluster bombs. Or we could have dwelt on the advantages for world peace of the American public adopting the Soviet gymnast Olga Korbut as their new hearthrob after the Munich Games. Finally, we could have concluded that modern, big-time sport, no matter how debased or tied up with politics or business it has become, is a good thing. Many eminent commentators have already proposed that thesis and we felt that it was time to state the other, no less valid, side of the argument. In doing so we may have appeared hostile to the concept of international sport or as passionate enemies of Communism.

This book has attempted to define, describe and explain the way that politics pervades Communist sport and how it has shaped both performance and people. It is, we feel, a contribution, however modest, to the great debate about the future of international sport.

SIMON FREEMAN AND ROGER BOYES

Below:
Russia's V. Krepkina jumping to a world lon jump record at Rome, 1960.

1 Changing Perspectives

In January 1964, a few months before the XVIII Olympiad opened in Tokyo, Mr. Rene Maheu, Director of the influential United Nations Educational, Scientific and Cultural Organisation (UNESCO) enthused over the role of the Olympics in cementing World peace. 'Quarrels, misunderstandings, conflicts and hatreds should be suspended during the Games. The combination of an eagerness to win and a respect for the rules which we find in sports competition leads naturally to greater mutual respect, understanding and even friendship. Yes, sport is a truce. In our technological societies ruled by the iron law of labor, in which man is only what he possesses and possesses only what he has earned, blessed is the game which fills our leisure time with riches. Amid the antagonisms and conflicts of our time which is dominated by the will to power and by pride, blessed is the respite which brings respect and friendship.' During the Munich Olympics eight years later Mr. Maheu was just as lyrical but his message was slightly different. Sportsmanship was being sacrificed as states sought success in sport. The world, he said, was forgetting the 'moral purpose' of sport. 'For the mass of people sport has become a form of entertainment of which they are mere spectators: radio and television spare them even the trouble of getting to the sportsground. The success of spectator sport and the importance it has come to assume in everyday life are unfortunately too often exploited for purposes alien or even opposed to sport – commercialism, chauvinism and politics – which corrupt and deform it. If we want to save sport's soul, the time has come to react and react quickly'.

It is not hard to understand why Mr. Maheu changed his mind. The Mexico Olympics in 1968 were a disaster; more memorable for rows about politics, sex tests, professionalism and commercialism than for athletic excellence or good humor. Munich was even more of a travesty. There was the tragic massacre of Israeli athletes by Palestinians, the forced withdrawal of the Rhodesian team and arguments about the influence of big business in what was, after all, supposed to be the World's premier amateur sports festival. In fact, all these incidents, dramatic though they were, were only part of a trend that could be traced back to 1936. The alarm bells had been tolling for sport since then; Mr. Maheu, like most people, had simply not heard them.

1936 marked the end of an era and a turning point for sport. Until then the gentlemen amateurs could, with some justification, claim that they had kept politics out of sport, which they believed should remain outside of and superior to more sordid human activities. But from the moment that it was announced that

Berlin would stage the XIth Olympiad it was clear that politics would dominate the games. 'An infamous festival dominated by Jews,' was how the Nazis summed up the Olympics when they heard the news. That, however, was in 1931 and they were still two years from power. In January 1933 Hitler seized control of the government and soon realised that the Games would be a marvellous way to bolster the glory of the Third Reich. He ordered government departments to release employees who were national squad members for full time training, and he increased the government budget for the festival fourteenfold. The capacity of the main Berlin stadium, built by the Kaiser in 1913, was enlarged from 60,000 to 100,000 and a luxurious Olympic village was built to house 4,000 athletes.

Western European and American sports officials – under fire from vocal anti-Nazi lobbies – watched the build-up with apprehension. They asked Hitler for assurances that all Germans, irrespective of race, religion or political creed, would be eligible for selection to the national team. The assurances were given and promptly ignored. The most infamous case of discrimination concerned the Jewish head of the German international Olympic committees. First he was forced to resign from the national athletic committee and then he came under pressure to resign from the Olympic organising committees. The IOC (International Olympic Committee), furious that their traditional role of controlling the festival was being threatened, stepped in and demanded that Hitler allow them to run the Games. As later events proved, Hitler's pledge was worthless.

In the months leading to the Games it became increasingly apparent that the IOC had been outmanoeuvred by the Nazis. The Olympics would, it seemed, be turned into a massive propaganda circus. There was talk of a boycott in the United States, which came to a head with a vote by the American National Olympic Committee. Luckily for Hitler, but unluckily for sport, the motion to boycott was defeated by 58 votes to 56. Leading the anti-boycott lobby was Avery Brundage, President of the IOC from 1952 to 1972 and ironically a fervent believer in the principle that politics should be kept out of sport.

Of course that did not happen when the Games opened on August 1, 1936. Western journalists watched, half in horror, half in admiration, as the opening ceremony, in theory a tribute to the brotherhood of nations, was transformed into a Nazi rally. Over 110,000 spectators crammed into the stadium, which was bedecked with hundreds of Nazi swastikas, to watch the athletes in the traditional march past. A military band thundered out stirring tunes, and a huge 14 ton bell rang out. As the fifty teams strode into the arena the crowd rose to their feet. The French were given a special cheer when they gave the raised arm Nazi salute to Hitler, who was predictably in full military dress. The British walked past Hitler and turned their eyes phlegmatically to the right. They were greeted in near silence. Bringing up the rear was the 500 strong German squad looking, many observers said later, more like a crack paratroop battalion than a team of athletes hoping to build peace through sport. Nothing had been left to chance. The athletes halted and with split second timing a blond runner – the Nazi's ideal Aryan youth – came into the arena holding the Olympic torch.

Hitler opens the Berlin Games.

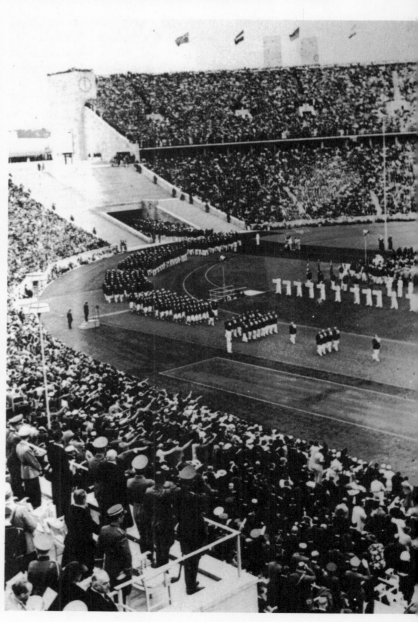

This had been lit in Greece and carried through Europe by almost 3,000 athletes. The torches, by the way, had been manufactured by the German arms firm of Krupps, at the time preoccupied with ensuring that the German army was the best equipped in the world. As thousands of doves were released the Olympic flame was lit and, as a final touch, Hitler was handed an olive branch by an ageing former marathon champion. The whole affair had been perfectly stage-managed, just as all Nazi rallies were.

'I suppose that the opening ceremony symbolised the fact that nations and national pride had become more important than individuals. There were flags and swastikas and troops everywhere. I didn't care for it much,' Sydney Wooderson, a member of the British squad that day, told the authors. Nearly half a century after

The Olympic flame is lit to open Hitler's Games.

Berlin, the Olympics are even more of a propaganda exercise; a tribute to nationalism rather than individualism, a battlefield for opposing political doctrines. 'As far as I can see the Moscow Games will be just the same as Berlin. The only difference will be that we know more about what is happening in Russia than we did about what was going on in Germany. Oh yes, and the athletes will be more professional and there will be millions of people watching on television. I wouldn't like to be an athlete today,' said Sydney. The similarities between Berlin and Moscow are certainly striking. Like Germany, the Soviet Union has a totalitarian regime. Soviet athletes will be told that they owe it to the Motherland to defeat the representatives of other political systems, just as Nazi athletes were urged to beat competitors from the 'decadent pro-Jewish democracies' and the 'black auxiliaries' of the United States. Success for Communist athletes in Moscow will be hailed as a victory for the system, just as the Nazis greeted every medal triumph in Berlin.

Was it inevitable that sport degenerated in this way? The writer and journalist George Orwell, author of classics like *1984* and *Animal Farm*, thought so. In 1945, shortly after the unhappy tour of England by the Russian Dynamo football team, he ridiculed the idea that sport could build friendship between nations.

'Sport is an unfailing cause of ill-will . . . and how could it be otherwise? I am always amazed when I hear people saying that sport creates goodwill between the nations, and that if only the common peoples of the world could meet one another at football or cricket, they would have no inclination to meet on the battlefield. Even if one didn't know from concrete examples (the 1936 Olympic Games, for instance) that international sporting contests lead to orgies of hatred, one could deduce it from general principles'. At the highest level, he continued, sport was 'frankly mimic warfare'. Serious sport has nothing to do with fair play. 'It is bound up with hatred, jealousy, boastfulness, disregard of all rules and sadistic pleasure in witnessing violence: in other words it is war minus the shooting'. Post-war industrial society, with its huge, bored urban populations, meant, said Orwell, that more and more people would have to indulge in the vicarious violence of sport. And that feeling would be most intense when national teams were playing. 'There cannot be much doubt that the whole thing is bound up with the rise in nationalism – that is, with the lunatic habit of identifying with large power units and seeing everything in terms of competitive prestige'. His final words were strangely prophetic: 'If you wanted to add to the vast fund of ill-will existing in the world you could hardly do it better than by a series of football matches between Jews and Arabs, Germans and Czechs, Indians and British, Russians and Poles, and Italians and Yugoslavs, each match to be watched by a mixed audience of 100,000 spectators'. With the exception perhaps of the British and Indians national hatreds haven't changed much since 1945.

Russian Foreign Minister Molotov signing the controversial non-aggression pact with Nazi Germany in August 1939. German Foreign Minister Ribbentrop is at extreme left, flanked by Stalin.

Nationalism has, as Orwell predicted would, come to dominate major sports tour ments. Germany and Japan, the two 'gui nations, were not invited to the London Oly pics in 1948, although the Games were design ostensibly to heal the wounds of war. At Melbourne Games in 1956, the first to be held the Southern Hemisphere, the politics of natic alism again intruded. There was considera bitterness over the Russian invasion of Hunga and five countries – Iraq, the Netherlan Lebanon, Egypt and Spain – boycotted Games in protest at the British-French adventu in Suez. At the Mexico Olympics in 1968 Soviet Union was again under attack: this ti for its suppression of the liberal regime Alexander Dubcek in Czechoslovakia. Muni in 1972 was the setting for a row about Rhodes invited to attend by the IOC providing marched under the old colonial flag and reco nised the British national anthem. Their tea however, was forced to return home after t African states told the IOC they would boyc the games if the Rhodesians weren't sent pac ing.

But the Montreal Games four years later pr vided the backcloth for the most bitter ro about national pride ever seen at an Olympic In 1958 the People's Republic of China had wit drawn from the IOC in protest after that bod had recognised the Taiwanese Nation Olympic Committee as having control of spo throughout the island and mainland. A year lat the IOC had second thoughts and said th Taiwan could still compete in the Olympics long as it did not call itself the 'Republic of Chin But in 1976 the IOC swung again, reversed i earlier decision and decreed that in Montre the Taiwanese team could legitimately call itse the 'Republic of China'. The Canadian gover ment, anxious not to jeopardize improving rela tions with China, announced that Taiwan wou be very welcome at Montreal, but not if the called their team the 'Republic of China'. Th Taiwanese, piqued at the prospective loss national face, withdrew. But this was not the en of the jingoistic haggling. The black Africa states, who had already repeated the Munic tactic and forced the IOC to withdraw an invita tion to Rhodesia, turned their attentions to Ne Zealand. They demanded that she, too, b thrown out of the Olympic movement for main taining sporting ties with the apartheid regim in South Africa. The IOC, for once, did n buckle and over 20 African states, despite plea to reconsider from the United Nations an Commonwealth Secretaries-General, refused t take part in the Games.

Incidents like this were not just confined to the Olympics. Taking top-class football as an example the same decline was also visible. In 1954 the Hungarians and Brazilians slugged it out in the dressing rooms after a particularly nasty World Cup match. In 1962 FIFA, the international soccer authority, pleaded with the World Cup teams of Germany, Argentina, Bulgaria, Chile and Italy to show restraint after a series of unpleasant matches. Two years later the Peru-Argentina match in Lima exploded into a full-scale riot after a last minute equalizer by Peru was disallowed. 318 people died and a further 500 were seriously hurt as fans made their feeling known. Later that day the crowd marched to the Presidential Palace and demanded an inquiry into the police tactics at the stadium. They called also for the match to be declared a draw.

The 1966 World Cup in England also did little to help international relations. The England team manager Alf Ramsey, later knighted for his services to sport, described the Argentinians as 'animals' after a foul-ridden match at Wembley Stadium. The remark has never been forgotten by the Argentinians. In June 1969 the trend reached its logical conclusion when the South American states of Honduras and El Salvador met in a soccer match. The result was that El Salvador declared war on Honduras. From then on nothing could have surprised the football authorities. During the African Games in 1978 the Egyptians and Libyans settled politican differences by brawling on the football field and after the World Cup that year both the Italian and Brazilian teams, who failed to satisfy the chauvinism of the fans, were stoned when they returned home. By the beginning of the 1980s sport rarely improved relations between countries and often seriously exacerbated them. Nor was it regarded, if it ever had been, by the politicians as an arena in which they had no part to play: 'Sport is not an end in itself,' said the Secretary General of the Organisation of African Unity after the Montreal walkout.

What has been the reaction of the sports authorities to these boycotts, rows and riots? After Montreal the IOC said limply that sanctions against the Africans would be 'counter-productive'. Lord Killanin, President of the IOC, said it was obvious that 'the politicians have taken over'. He added: 'It may be a pious and ideal hope, but we hope that after what happened at Montreal no government will close the door to any Olympic athlete or at least if it does, will give us adequate warning so that other

RUSSIAN
MATCH
ABANDONED

TICKETS REFUNDED BY POST ONLY

Russian athletes visiting London in 1956 had a head-on collision with the politics of sport. The team's champion women's discus thrower was accused of shoplifting from a London store: Soviet officials treated the incident as a sinister plot to discredit Russian womanhood and the team walked out on a scheduled athletics meeting.

arrangements can be made.' In other words, nothing could be done to take the nationalism out of sport.

The increasing importance of international sport has meant that political or 'sub national' groups as well as governments have been able to use major tournaments for their own purposes. The first notable political protest of the post-war Olympics came at Helsinki in 1952 when a 23 year old girl from West Germany ran into the arena during the opening ceremony, mounted the rostrum, seized the microphone and delivered a speech about the need for world peace. In 1968 the Mexico Games were overshadowed by local students protesting – many felt with some justice – about the massive cost of staging the festival. How, they asked, could their government find money for sport but not for new homes, schools or hospitals? The American negro sprinters Tommie Smith and John Carlos also felt the Games were a suitable platform to air political grievances. Climbing onto the winners' rostrum after Smith's victory in the 200 metres both men raised black-gloved hands to the sky in the familiar 'Black Power' salute of American negroes. Shortly before he was sent home in disgrace Smith said that his gold medal had highlighted the paradoxical position of successful black athletes. 'If I win I'm an American, not a black American. If I did something bad then I would just be a negro.'

Munich, of course, was the scene for the most infamous political protest of all. 'A bomb in the White House, a mine in the Vatican, the death of Mao-Tse-Tung, an earthquake in Paris, could not

have echoed through the consciousness of every man, in the world like the operation in Munich. It was like painting the name of Palestine on the top of a mountain that can be seen from the four corners of the earth . . .' wrote one Arab newspaper, after the Black September killing of 11 Israelis. The episode was especially poignant because the West Germans had desperately wanted the Games to be remembered as the 'carefree Olympics'; to prove that they had at last shrugged off the martial habits of the 1930s. Later a Palestinian spokesman apologised to the sportsmen of the world: 'But we want them to know of the existence of a people whose country has been occupied for 24 years and their honour trampled underfoot . . . There is no harm that the world understands their tragedy for a few hours . . . so let the Games stop for a few hours.'

The Black September massacre was a heinous enough crime in its own right and would have inevitably provoked protests, from friends as well as enemies of the Palestinian Liberation Organisation. But because many people had clung to the belief that sport was divorced from grubby political realities the reaction was doubly strong. The Palestinians were attacked both because of the crime itself and because they had shown, once and for all, that the sanctity of sport was a thing of the past. 'It was an intrusion of human conflict on one of those universal rites of modern man, which by sublimating it, supposedly help prevent it. The breaking of the Olympic peace was a kind of sacrilege . . .' wrote one British journalist in his study of the Arab-Israeli conflict. Other journalists felt even more outraged: 'Such an attack on one of the most generous ideas of the 20th Century, this attack on the Olympic ideal, the fraternal gathering of the elite of the world's youth, seems to be an additional crime, equally to be condemned . . .'; 'a breach of the Olympic peace . . .', this barbaric invasion is a threat to the future of the Games . . .'; 'we have seen the assassination of a myth.' Newspapers were swamped with vitriolic letters attacking the entire Arab race and in many towns throughout Europe Arabs were banned from shops and restaurants. One wonders if the response would have been so powerful had the murdered Israelis been businessmen attending a conference.

The Munich tragedy meant that all major sports events in the future would be as much about security as sport. At the Winter Olympics in Innsbruck in 1976 the French newspaper *Le Monde* said that the Olympic village was like a fortified camp. 'The security measures for Innsbruck are impressive. Two thousand five

...rs flow for the ...aelis and the ideals ...t died at Munich. The ...urner with the large ...ndkerchief is Jesse ...ens.

hundred security officers, including policemen, soldiers, and even specially recruited private detectives are on duty... There are five policeman for every athlete. The Olympic village has been turned into a real stronghold. It is surrounded by a high fence fitted with alarm systems and lit up all night long by powerful searchlights. The entrance is guarded round the clock and no one can get past without all the necessary passes. An electronic detection system, similar to those used at airports, enables the guards to detect the presence of any arms. If, for example, a journalist wishes to meet an athlete he is accompanied by a police officer right up to the cafe of the athletic section. There, a hostess goes to find the athlete he wishes to see. All personalities are permanently protected by the state police. Their official cars are driven by security agents. The huge array of security forces is completed by an anti-terrorist squad, an arsenal of various kinds of arms, a hundred radio cars and several helicopters. And finally there are special checks at the Austrian frontier'. The total budget for security was estimated to be 30 million Austrian schillings. One Austrian police official said as he surveyed the fences and guards: 'The best possible form of security measures requires a visible presence. The peaceful image of the Games is bound to take a bit of a knock'.

Before the Summer Games in Montreal administrators insisted that security would be allowed to ruin the atmosphere of the festi 'We have every intention of presenting to world an Olympic Games worthy of man, wi proper balance between the spirit and the re ity, rewarding to the present generation a beneficial to generations of the future', said Roger Rousseau, President and Commissio of the Organising Committee of the Gam Mayor Drapeau confessed that he knew 'a about terrorists' and pledged that Montr would not be turned into 'an armed camp'.

Naturally, the reverse happened. the Ca dian government, more worried about Fren Canadian terrorists than Palestinians, moun the biggest security operation since the Seco World War, at an estimated cost of £70 milli Most journalists returned home complain that whilst the Games had been as safe as po ible they had been spoilt by the massive secu presence. There are, however, no fears o terrorist outrage in Moscow in 1980. Fi because of the extraordinarily tight border c trols, which would confound the most enterp ing terrorist and which, for once, will be used prevent people getting into the Soviet Un rather than getting out. Second, because there no danger from Soviet-based terrorists, w simply do not exist. In the months before ames, the KGB made sure that human rights ctivists would not cause any embarrassing cidents by exiling known dissidents from oscow.

If it is certain that Moscow will not be used by ay terrorist group to publicise its aims it is qually certain that the Games will be used by e Communist regimes of Eastern Europe and uba to justify their political system. Victory for eir competitors will be saluted as a victory for ommunism over Capitalism. This rivalry has, in ct, been a crucial factor in influencing the evelopment of sport since the Second World ar and it has slowly forced the Western demo- acies to view sport as a test of ideologies as uch as a test of nations. For instance, one ench commentator said after his team's poor erformance at Innsbruck: 'It's the worst rout for years . . . what a comedown in such a short ne'. The politicians were even more infuriated: sports enthusiast cannot help but be dis- essed by the poor results obtained by our ational teams. No, it is not the athletes' fault. We ccuse the government sports policy . . . Sports culcate a fighting spirit and teaches endur- ace. So when we see France bringing up the ar in international competition, that is further

proof that in every field the time has come for a change of policy'.

During the late fifties and early sixties the West watched in bewilderment as the Commun- ist states of Eastern Europe swept all before them in major sports events. Gradually, though, information on how this success was being achieved began to filter through the Iron Cur- tain. Newspapers like the German *Der Spiegel* published secret training manuals illustrating how the Communists were selecting promising children and giving them specialised training. 'Preparation for the Olympic Games must start before school age. If we can convince creche and nursery school teachers of this it should be possible to analyse the development of the child over a period of at least three years before he goes to school and thereby obtain information needed to improve his sports education,' *Der Spiegel* quoted from the report. Another report revealed that the East Germans had set up a 'national sports card system', whereby cards containing the physical and sports record of every athlete were fed into a central computer. Yet another story quoted this East German memorandum: It is essential to start selection early, in the first or second year of school,

A symbol for Moscow.

The Republic of China (Taiwan) Olympic Attaché announcing that his country would not be allowed to compete in Montreal, 1976, because of political pressure from the Canadian Government.

otherwise there is a danger that children will become interested in subjects or get into circles that have nothing to do with sport! There was, too, growing evidence through the sixties and seventies of widespread abuse of drugs by Communist athletes.

Not surprisingly, there have been demands by many Western athletes for more government support. How else, they asked, can they be expected to compete against the Communists? So far, democratic governments have not responded but there has been sufficient encroachment by the state to prompt protests from old-fashioned idealists. IOC President Lord Killanin said after the Montreal Olympics: 'Being from Ireland I have come to the Olympics with more than one team that did not win a gold medal. I was neither sad nor happy. Sometimes you would have thought that the Ministers of Sport of some countries and not their athletes had won the medals by the way they have been hopping about and kissing each other.' Journalist Christopher Brasher, a former British Olympic athlete, pointed out that: '20 years ago hardly a country in the world had a Minister of Sport. Even New Zealand, whose government wins elections on the platform which includes the phrase, no political interference in sport, has a Minister of Sport'. In the summer of 1979 Prince Philip told a London audience that he had no patience with those people who wanted more government support and control of sport. Sport should not be, he continued, a way of gaining international prestige. it should rather be about enjoying oneself and, if necessary, learning to lose gracefully.

In fact, these grumbling Western athletes ar no longer being entirely candid when they sa that they have no chance against the stat supported Communist 'professionals'. In rece years the IOC have relaxed the rules governir the amount of full-time training and cash bac] ing amateurs can enjoy without endangerir their status. Of course, the Americans ha always found a way around these regulations I awarding college sports scholarships to ou standing performers. The change in the IO rules means that athletes in other countries, lil West Germany, Britain and France, are al competing on more equal terms with the Con munists. Much of the money needed to he them comes from big business – which has bee quick to spot the enormous commercial pote tial of an association with international sport

Some change in the IOC rules was inevitab] During the 70s there were frequent rows abo illegal payments to athletes by companies, wl simply asked that the sportsmen wear or u their equipment. Skiing – an expensive sport which there is intense competition betwee sportswear and equipment manufacturers – w often at the centre of these arguments. Befo the Winter Olympics in Sapporo in 1972 tl French newspaper *Le Monde* commented: 'S manufacturers are determined to use the Gam to exploit the Japanese market. What is at sta] is the biggest winter sports market in the worl The sale of no less than 16 million pairs of skis up for grabs and all that goes with it! One m chievous journalist calculated that the averag French Olympic skier earned about $35,0 from under the counter payments.

Until he stepped down from the IOC pre dency Avery Brundage did his best to stop tl Olympics being taken over by big business. 1971 he said that he would ban athletes wl 'allow their names or photographs to be used f the purpose of advertising sports equipmen clothing'. If they did this then, said Brundag they would become professionals. Who wou have thought, he lamented on another occasio that sport would become a means for 'promotir tourism, sports equipment and sportswea Even if one sympathised with Brundage's idea ism it was obviously too late, as one newspap pointed out: 'If Brundage's rules were applie then 90 per cent of the athletes taking part in tl games would have to be disqualified!

By the summer of 1979 many Western athlete were in full-time training for the 1980 Olympic British athletes like Sebastian Coe, Wor] record holder in the mile, could look forward a year of preparation without having to wor about earning a living. The money came from

Above Left:
Street scene from Olympic village in Munich after the terrorists had struck.

Above:
The terrorist's handiwork.

The Munich tragedy may have changed the atmosphere of the Olympics for ever.

Viktor Korchnoi lodges
a complaint about an
alleged
parapsychologist
planted in the audience
by the KGB to disrupt
his 1978 bid to win the
world chess
championship from
Karpov.

variety of sources: from the Sports Aid Foundation, an independent and privately funded body with a multi-million pound budget; from altruistic companies; from lotteries and even from concerts given by pop stars. Other athletes were given paid leave by their firms. Sprinter Donna Hartley, for instance, was allowed six months off work by her employers, the Midland Bank. Mr. Alan Weeks, a BBC sports commentator and director of the foundation, said that British athletes would no longer have to fret about

money. 'We believe that those thinking abo money and suffering financially for their spo are not in the right frame of mind to succeed. I our intention that this should not be possible Britain again' Skater Robin Cousins was obv ously pleased with the new arrangements: 'F the first time I'm able to do everything I want. don't have to call home anymore to chec whether we can afford it. And I don't have worry about the sacrifices my folks are makin All I have to worry about is skating'.

This does not mean that amateur sport ha put its house in order. 'Shamateurism' – the flou ing of the rules by amateur athletes in return fo money – is still very much with us. At the Europ Cup match in Turin in the summer of 197 athletes were the target for countless agents an salesmen waving chequebooks and promisin small fortunes in return for minor, but illega favours. Most people now recognise tha nothing can be done to stop this. The only sol tion, and this was being considered widely i 1979, would be to abolish the professiona amateur distinction – as has happened in tenni

Since the war the administrators have had ye another problem to grapple with – the eve increasing cost and size of the great peripateti sports tournaments. 'Major sports meetings lik the Olympics,' one French economist wrote 'require a high mobilisation of capital. Hug financial resources are required ... and sma countries, especially in the Third World, cann last the pace of this sports rivalry.' In 1970 th Dutch Minister for Culture, Sport and Leisure pu it even more succinctly: 'The organisation of th Olympics requires financial sacrifices which ar beyond the means of a small country like min Glasgow, which had been hoping to stage th 1984 or 1988 Games, took heed of this and swiftl dropped the idea. The most conservative esti mates for staging the Games in the city had bee £450 million.

None of the changes we have discussed – th growth of nationalism, the threat of terrorism the challenge of 'shamateurism' – would hav occurred without television. Without televisio the sports stage would not have widened t encompass, on occasions, vast chunks of Man kind. Without television sport might well hav stayed rooted in the Halcyon days of th gentlemen amateurs.

Television now dominates lives in both th West and East. By 1974, for example, two thirds c Soviet families had their own television sets. B 1980 televised sport had become such big busi ness that the NBC American network had pai over $80 million for the rights to show the Mos cow Games.

Newspapers, too, played their part in promoting the growth of sport. Technical developments meant that news could be flashed around the world in minutes and printed in time for the next day's morning papers. In both the West and East the public's appetite for sport seemed insatiable: in the Soviet Union alone the circulation of the top sports journals more than trebled between 1962 and 1973.

Unhappily, sportswriters and television sports commentators have, on the whole, ducked the responsibilities that have come with their new found stature. In the West, with the exception of a few quality writers and broadcasters, crude jingoism and sensationalism are still the staple diet of sports fans. In Communist countries the public are clearly worse off with their diet of political propaganda and selective sports results. During the Chinese soccer team's tour of England in the summer of 1979 it was clear that most journalists have learnt little over the years. The Chinese were adopted as the new 'cuties' of world sport, much as Olga Korbut had been adopted as the girl we all ought to love after her appearances at the Munich Olympics in 1972.

But the greatest disservice that the media has done to sport has been to take it all too seriously. During the Munich Games one young West German student decided that a little bit of fun was needed. He ran into the stadium, where the crowd were anxiously awaiting the arrival of the marathon runners, was greeted with cheers, then silence as the confused officials tried to discover who he was. Meanwhile the actual runners had started to arrive – without the traditional welcome accorded marathon men. 'The purpose of my act was to protest against the solemnity, seriousness and over-organisation of the Games,' said the student later. The newspapers were furious: 'This usurper of glory deprived us of those few priceless seconds when the crowd rises to acclaim the most deserved of victories. Emotion gave way to farce. It will take a long time to get over our disappointment.' Perhaps the world would do well to recall the words of American sportswriter Red Smith: 'Knock off the hypocrisy, stop telling kids what an honor it is to represent their country and give them a chance to play games for the fun of it. Maybe it would work.'

2 The History of Communist Success

In Sofia, when the Russian ice skaters Irina Rodnina and Alexander Zaitsev have left the rink, heard their results and go towards their changing rooms to rub down, they are immediately surrounded by Bulgarian schoolgirl fans wanting an autograph. It is the skaters' one moment of vulnerability: the one time when they are not dogged by coach, trainer, chaperone or security guard. From their brief unforced smiles it is clear that they enjoy their celebrity. The effect is much the same in the rest of Eastern Europe. Russia provides the stars, like tennis player Olga Marozova, weightlifter Vasily Alexeyev and the Communist allies look on admiringly.

That at least is one half of the story. But such scenes disguise the hard edge of competition which exists between Russia and Eastern European countries in the sport arena. We discuss (chapter three) the ideological 'X' factor and the network of special training institutes (chapter six) which can help the Communist countries to victory over the West. It is too often forgotten by Western sports commentators, however, that there is a deep and sometimes bitter rivalry between the Eastern European countries themselves – a rivalry which can only be explained by looking at the origins of sports in the various countries.

There are of course the more obviously political grudges. Encounters between Rumania and Hungary for example have been particularly sharp over the past few years because of a row over Rumania's treatment of the Hungarian minority in Transylvania. Matches between East Germany and Poland also have an undercurrent of bitterness: The GDR may be an ally now but memories of the Second World War (many of the major concentration camps were in Poland) are still strong.

Sport provides a useful and apparently harmless way of expressing nationalist sentiments. The most trenchant example of this is the regular ice hockey encounter between the Soviet Union and Czechoslovakia. Since the invasion of Czechoslovakia in 1968 the match (usually in the world championship) has taken on special significance especially as the Czech team is currently stronger than the Russian side. For the Czech spectators at the rink-side or in front of the TV it provides a legitimate excuse to shout anti-Russian slogans.

But there are more profound differences between the East European countries than sim-

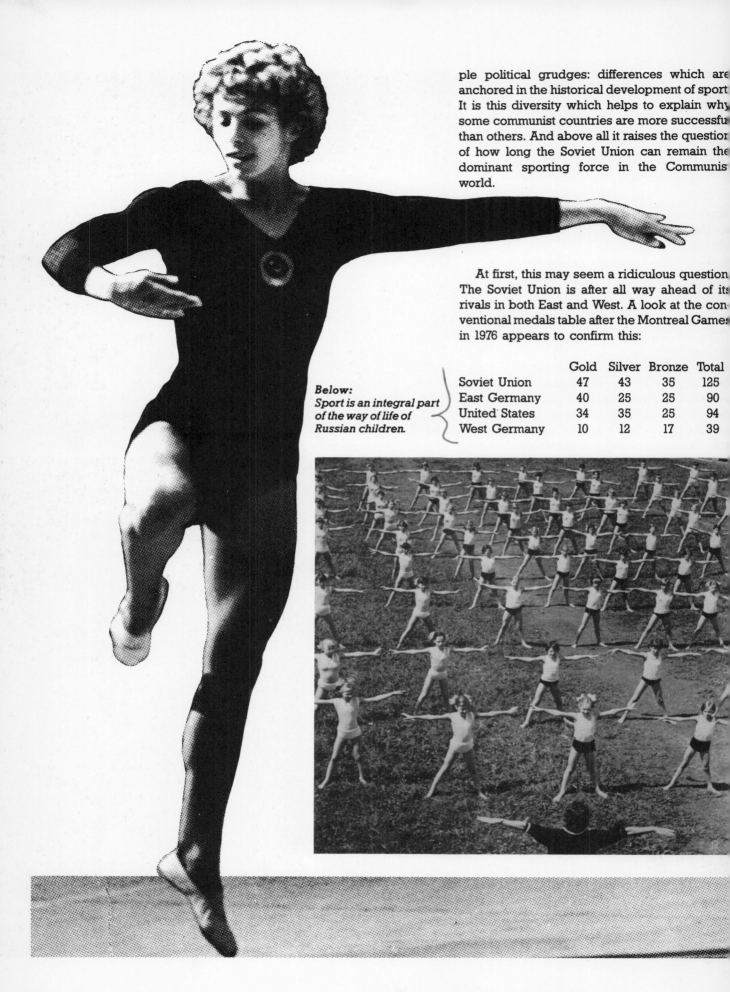

ple political grudges: differences which are anchored in the historical development of sport. It is this diversity which helps to explain why some communist countries are more successful than others. And above all it raises the question of how long the Soviet Union can remain the dominant sporting force in the Communist world.

At first, this may seem a ridiculous question. The Soviet Union is after all way ahead of its rivals in both East and West. A look at the conventional medals table after the Montreal Games in 1976 appears to confirm this:

Below:
Sport is an integral part of the way of life of Russian children.

	Gold	Silver	Bronze	Total
Soviet Union	47	43	35	125
East Germany	40	25	25	90
United States	34	35	25	94
West Germany	10	12	17	39

But if we now adjust the table in terms of population, a good indicator of relative strength, then a rather different picture emerges. In medals per million of population, the smaller East European countries and Cuba are well up in the table.

	Total Medals	Pop. (Millions)	Medals per million
Bermuda	1	0.05	20.00
East Germany	90	16.98	5.30
Bulgaria	24	8.62	2.78
Hungary	21	10.41	2.02
Cuba	13	8.87	1.50
New Zealand	4	2.96	1.35
Rumania	27	20.83	1.30

The smaller communist countries are significantly ahead of the Soviet Union (20th), West Germany (13th) and the U.S.A. (22nd). What does this prove? In the first place, it shows that the breadth of interest in sport in Eastern Europe must have existed long before the countries took on Soviet-type systems. Countries with such scanty resources as Bulgaria could not produce these kind of results as a consequence of just three decades of communism, although this clearly was a strong factor.

Second, the table shows that the true challenge to Soviet sport in the late 1980's and 1990's will come from East Germany and Cuba. The relative success of Rumania and Bulgaria have come about from a blend of sporting tradition with extreme specialisation. By concentrating its financial resources on gymnastics and only a few other sports, Rumania has guaranteed itself an important place on the medal table as has Bulgaria by focusing on athletics, especially field events. But the real challenge comes from East Germany and, in a more philosophical way,

Above:
Chess grabs the Russian imagination from an early age.

Right:
A pupil at the Olympic Reserve School in Moscow preparing a netball throw.

Below:
The Marmi Stadium in the early stages of construction for the 1960 Olympics. Where else but Rome?

Cuba. Both these countries have a rapidly rising birth rate – providing an ever-expanding reserve of talent – while the USSR has a diminishing birth rate. This is especially the case in the European part of Russia – which still provides the bulk of the Soviet Olympic side. Only in the Moslem areas of Soviet Central Asia is the population still increasing – but Central Asians are still significantly under-represented in Soviet teams.

The strength of East Germany and Cuba lies too in their historical traditions and their openness to new sporting concepts from the West. This is not to suggest though that Cuba will ever push the Soviet Union from first position: its challenge is a more abstract one, showing that it is not necessary to have vast resources to be a strong sporting power. East Germany, on the other hand, could well displace the Soviet Union in the medals table – although some Sovietologists have suggested that it will rein in its sporting efforts before it gets to that stage. While the Soviet Union dominates the political complexion of Eastern Europe, it is wise for the East Germans and other countries to play a diplomatic second fiddle.

It is logical then to look at the origins of East German and Cuban sport to see from where they draw their long-term strength. We shall also briefly examine the roots of Chinese sport.

Although Peking is still insignificant in the international sporting arena it has the seeds of success for the 21st Century: it has a long history of mass and elite sport, a large and growing population, considerable financial resources and, now that the Gang of Four leadership has been ousted, a strong urge to do well in international competition.

East Germany: 'From *Turnmeister* to robot-sport'.

It would be difficult to think of three more different countries than East Germany, Cuba and China: they are different in size, continent and temperament. Even their forms of Communism are different: strongly Soviet in the GDR, woven around the personality of Castro in Cuba and loosely pragmatic though passionately anti-Russian in China. But in their sporting traditions there are common links – links which one day could well make them three of the most dominant sporting powers in the world.

One of these common links is their response to Western influence in terms of new sports, new techniques and the acceptance of healthy competition. The same openness could not be attributed to the Soviet Union which, after the 1917 revolution, resisted any serious contact with the

The Sports Palace in Luzhniki being adapted to house the gymnastics and judo competitions for the Moscow Games. No expense has been spared in an effort to top the extravaganzas of Montreal and Munich.

The Lenin Stadium in Moscow.

West. Moscow's first official sports agreement with the West was with Nazi Germany in the late '30s but in general it has shunned exchanges and shared facilities apart from connections with other Communist countries.

In Germany by contrast sport was at the beginning an open affair. In 1836 for example an 'English rowing club' was established in Hamburg and other towns followed suit. The initial shaping influence came earlier however – from the threat of invasion by Napoleon. The plan, as outlined by Germany's leading sports philosopher Friedrich 'Turnmeister' Jahn was to give young Prussians pre-military training and to blend this with normal organised sporting activity: ever since then German sport has had a distinctly militaristic and regimented flavor and this in turn has influenced the complexion of Soviet sport.

The official mood swung for and against Jahn over the years like a democratic barometer. After Napoleon was defeated his sports organisations were considered to be subversive: they encouraged to a limited extent the mixing of classes, and there was much discussion about political liberation through sport. It was allowed to function again after the unsuccessful democ-

ratic revolution of 1848 but the two strands of the Jahn philosophy – democracy and national unity under Prussian control – seemed to be at odds and eventually dulled the impact of the so-called *Turnverein* movement on modern German sport.

Germany looked abroad for possible models of how sport should be organised. Under British influence the Germans set up organisations for swimming, cycling, sailing, athletics, rugby and soccer. On the British model too, the main participants were drawn from the middle class. None the less the middle class was broadly based in Germany after unification and some real talent was unveiled, above all in gymnastics and swimming. It was during this period indeed that swimming and gymnastics began to be seen as 'natural' German sports – indeed the East Germans are still well ahead of the Soviet Union in many swimming events, though the Russians (partly through studying German techniques) are back on the upswing.

In the early 1900s a German Olympic movement was set up and in 1912 the Germans participated with a 185 strong team at the Stockholm games. They put up a creditable performance for a comparatively young nation – five golds,

Cuba's Teofilo Stevenson won his second consecutive gold in heavyweight boxing at Montreal.

Tamara Press, Russia's legendary shot-putt champion of the sixties, in action.

fourteen silver and six bronze medals. This w
still somewhat behind Britain but most sig
ficanly, the U.S. carried off most of the meda
This impressed the Germans considerably an
from then on British influence tended to wan
while interest in the U.S. rose.

The German papers were near-ecstatic
their admiration for the Americans. 'America
race with their heads as well as their legs, an
their Olympic victories are won on the pla
grounds of their schooldays;' the *Vossiscl
Zeitung*, a Berlin newspaper, commented. No
the reference to school days: it was as early
1912 that the Germans realised that they wou
have to start selection and training at a muc
earlier age than was normal in the country at th
time.

In the close contacts between Nazi German
and the Soviet Union in the late 1930s and ear
1940s (that is during the time of the Ribbe
trop/Molotov pact and before Hitler's invasion
Russia) this idea was transmitted to the Sovi
Russians, who, after the war, decided to app
the approach.

During the period between the two war
sport in Germany took on an increasingly polit
cal tone. The two main foreign influences
German sport had concentrated, in the Britis
case, on amateur sport supervised within a fair
relaxed framework, and in the US case on shar
competition. But German sport became mor
and more associated with patriotism and milita
ism and political factionalism. This was part
the consequence of the troubled Weima
Republic which was breaking up into separat

Imost ungovernable units – political parties like he Social Democrats (who eventually claimed ome two million members) started their own nass sports movements to attract recruits.

Out of this environment came Hitler. Many Germans thought that he would rescue them rom the apparently sordid political wheeler-dealing of the Weimar Republic. Instead he created a form of cult politics which enshrined patriotism and militarism and disguised more problems than it solved. That too was the fate of port which became a way of 'proving' the racial dominance of the Aryan.

The supreme symbol of Nazi sport was the 936 Olympics. There the amateur professional distinction was well and truly swept aside: portsmen and trainers were given several months free from work to train and prove the uperiority of the Third Reich. The IOC insisted n foreign teams of all nationalities being allowed to enter the Olympics and Hitler agreed even to allow a few Jews into the German side despite the country's anti-semitic policies. The ews were however little more than a token: most of them were not allowed into the Nazi-organised sports associations and so did not even come into the reckoning for Olympic election.

The East German sporting style has a few common elements with the Nazi Games: the ame love of propaganda trappings, the ban-ers and display, the same blend of politics with nternational competition. Emigrés claim that ome of the racialism has stayed on from the 930s but although there are racialist trends

(working tacitly against the Central Asians and Jews) in Soviet sport, there is not much evidence to suggest that the same happens in East Germany.

Rather, the East German approach towards the Nazi roots of its sport machine is a little shame-faced. East Germans we interviewed tended to say things like 'it couldn't happen again' – although the Communist Party is perva-sive, it hasn't permeated society as the Nazi sys-tem did in the 1930s. The East Germans are confident that their long tradition of sport will outweigh the legacy of the Nazi period and will be the foundation of future sporting victories.

Left:
Cuba's Alberto Juantorena winning the 800 metres at Montreal.

Right:
East Germany's Kornelia Ender winning the 100 m butterfly at Montreal to equal her own world record of 1:00.13.

The legendary Jesse Owens doing what he did best: winning.

Above:
The 'ping-pong diplomats': after one of its excursions into the world of international sport in the early seventies, China's tennis team plays host to a British team on a return visit.

The earliest known photo of soccer played in Russia, taken outside Moscow in 1881.

Hungary's gold medal fencing team at the Stockholm Games 1952.

ba: Independence through Sport

The first man in the modern history of the mpics to win three individual gold medals beit at separate games) was the Cuban fencer non Fonst. Unfortunately, we cannot pretend t this was a token of the dazzling sporting dition of Cuba: Fonst was the first and last man win gold medals for Cuba until Fidel Castro k over the small Caribbean island in 1959. But re are other measures of Cuba's sporting dition than the Olympics. It has a breadth of erest which embraces sports like baseball, xing, gymnastics, swimming and basketball. stro is fond of saying that before he took over, rt was a rich man's preserve which eroded national sports performance. This is only tly true. Certainly this is true of the tradition- elite sports like tennis (in which Cuba did l during the regional Pan-American Games) ich required good facilities but the lower sses, especially in the sugar plantations, wed a natural talent for games like basket-

ball. This did however lead to an imbalance: in the 1930s and 1940s, the talented working class basketball and baseball players and boxers would go to the USA and turn professional thus escaping the dreadful poverty.

Castro, for all his public utterances, has understood this use of sport as social betterment and tried to use it to the advantage of Cuba. Thus he has banned professional sport, but given special privileges and pay to top sportsmen to persuade them that it is in their interests not to drift towards the USA. In any case, emigration has been made extremely difficult, especially for talented sportsmen. While this may seem an intrusion, a curtailment of elementary liberties – the freedom to turn professional and the free-dom to emigrate – it has met with surprisingly little opposition from the bulk of the island's athletes.

There is no question of Cuban sportsmen defecting in the same way that Soviet or East German athletes do. Partly this is because of a personal loyalty to Castro, but partly too it is because of an awareness of the Cuban sporting tradition without which they cannot function. This is not a closed tradition (again as in the Soviet Union) but rather one that draws its strength from the example of overseas athletes and competitors. Cuba has been participating in the Central American and Caribbean Games since the 1920s and has dominated them for some time. The basic component for Cuba's sporting background is great racial diversity (it has a population of nine million) with Spanish

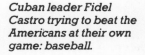

Cuban leader Fidel Castro trying to beat the Americans at their own game: baseball.

Left:
A Russian goal during an ice hockey tussle against Czechoslovakia.

33

and African influences predominating. The black cultural influence especially has given them a natural advantage over other Central American rivals like Venezuela and Mexico.

But the main influence on the early sporting history of Cuba was America. This was not just because of its attraction for budding professionals, nor simply because of the import of the poor man's sport, baseball. It was largely because of the so-called Pan-American Games which draws together North, Central and South America. The USA has naturally called the tune in these games from the beginning, even though it has often sent non-Olympic competitors. But the Cubans watched the Americans closely, quietly tried out some of the techniques, and on at least one proven occasion actually spied on the US delegation to see what their sportsmen were allowed to get up to after hours. By 1975,

Cuba was finishing second after the U.S. and ahead of Canada in the Pan-American unofficial medals table.

Since Castro took over, the Soviet and Eastern Bloc influence has displaced Western influences to some degree. The Russians have helped to build facilities, Polish trainers have been particularly successful with Cuban athletes. But despite Castro's claims the Eastern Bloc influence has not been the decisive factor in Cuba's remarkable sporting record. Instead it has been the result of a blend between the sport for all ideology and elitist ideologies and a recognition that there are lessons to be learnt from the country's own past and from other countries. It is a winning combination for a country with virtually no economic strength – and it is a lesson that the Russians would do well to study.

In both Cuba and East Germany we are talk-

Communist China ventures into the international sports arena: its national soccer team plays the Chelsea club team on tour of Britain, 1979.

ing in terms of a sporting tradition which goes back at most two centuries. In China sport interest can be traced back almost 4,000 years; there are signs of Chinese hunting, swimming, running. Even football was played in China as early as the fourth century BC – with a round leather ball stuffed with hair and feathers. Polo, archery and hockey were also played in China long before many countries were discovered.

The main influence on China's early sports tradition was religion. This tended to push physical exercise into the background and emphasised the benefits of mental training. This blended well with some sports – notably the martial arts. The Shaolin monasteries used the self-defence movements – popularised recently under the term Kung Fu (from 'Gong Fu' which simply means exercise) – as a way of improving

monks' health. As the Shaolin monastic discipline banned meat, sex, irregular habits and any stimulants including tea, the exercise must have provided a useful outlet for aggressive drives. But on the whole the doctrines of Confucianism, Taoism and Buddhism tended to minimise the importance of physical drives and indeed stressed friendship, contemplation and withdrawal from competition.

It was through the West – and indeed through the unlikely vehicle of the Young Men's Christian Association (YMCA) that sport was discovered in China. At missionary schools which were widespread throughout China in the mid and late 19th Century, Western priests organised baseball, table tennis, volleyball and gymnastics competitions. The YMCA had the advantage of supplying a ready-made organisational framework which could be super-imposed on the country. 'Christianity especially the muscular YMCA brand was the best thing that could have happened for Chinese sport,' said China-watcher David Dodwell, 'otherwise, given the highly individualist culture of the Chinese, competitive games might never have got restarted.'

There is something in what Dodwell says. As early as 1915 the YMCA was running a training programme in China for its own sports directors and soon these were active in most of the major provinces in the country. Provincial and National championships were also introduced by the YMCA and the competitive spirit seemed to seize the young Chinese.

But as in East Germany and Cuba, the tide eventually turned away from the Westerners. The competitive spirit seemed to strengthen the undercurrents of nationalist pride: as the athlete proved himself on the sportsfield, local heroes grew up and gained political significance. In the 1920s Nationalist Chinese often adopted local Chinese sportsmen and held them up as models for the future rebellion: fit, clean-living, learning from the West but not becoming dependent on foreigners.

These then are the characteristics which bind such disparate Communist countries as Cuba and China. A willingness to learn from the West and to test themselves against strong foreign competition even when there is a good chance of losing. And at the same time a national pride which converts interest in sport into a heart-felt commitment to the state – which is not just a means to win privilege and financial improvement. There is, too, the continued ability to make sacrifices in sporting terms – making do with scarce training resources – if the state considers it necessary.

3 Ideology and Sports

Viktor Korchnoi, the former Soviet chess grandmaster, used to be a passionate poker player in his youth, much to the irritation of the USSR chess federation. During the world chess championships in the steamy Phillipines summer of 1978, Korchnoi showed clear traces of his old love; he would bluff and counter-bluff Anatoly Karpov, the world champion, and constantly take risks. But Korchnoi, the 48 year old Russian defector, ultimately lost 6-5 to the young Soviet champion. For all his poker-player intuition, Korchnoi could not in the end resist the Communist sports machine, that curious contraption made up of training, skill, political manoeuvre and yet more training.

But there is an additional ingredient in the Soviet recipe for success – ideology. It was this X-factor which ultimately cost the Russian defector the most important match of his life.

To the Western sportsman, winning means many things: personal achievement, honor and sometimes wealth. For Communist sportsmen, it means these things too (although the financial element clearly has a different significance) but it also symbolises the triumph of a system, their system. To see a Soviet sprinter flash past the winning post is the ultimate reassurance for the Russian people and the sportsmen themselves that their way of life is the correct one. Sportsmen are the true heroes in the Communist world, not soldiers or film stars.

All this may seem a little wishy-washy to the Western sports-fan. To an Englishman, the sight of Sharron Davies splashing her way to victory is an understandable cause of pride but the sensation is a momentary one: he is under no illusion that Britain has become more powerful or significant because it has won a couple of gold medals in a swimming tournament. But in the Soviet Union, in East Germany, indeed in all the East Bloc countries and Cuba, the reverse is the case. Not only is a gold medal a national triumph – it is concrete proof that the Communist system actually works better than the capitalist system does in the West.

On their own admission, the ideological motive is one of the prime driving forces behind such competitors as Anatoly Karpov, the world chess champion, the Russian gymnast Ludmilla Turishcheva, the East German sprinter Renate Stecher and the Cuban boxer Teofilo Stevenson. Even less-than-convinced Marxists like the former world chess champion Boris Spassky get caught up with the emotionally-charged compulsion to prove that their system is right.

The World chess championship in Reykjavik in 1972 which for the first time in modern chess history pitched an American, Bobby Fischer, against a Russian, Spassky, neatly illustrated a clash of systems.

Thanks to the unpredictable play of Fischer – which threw the Spassky's back-up team completely off balance – and his unsettling match tactics (he threatened to withdraw several times), the Soviet chess machine faltered. For the first time since 1937, a non-Russian became world champion. The turnabout caused great confusion in Moscow and the ripples were felt throughout Soviet sport and not just in the chess federation. Trainers were fired, funds flowed into the coffers of the chess organisations to make sure it could not happen again, and Boris Spassky, the amiable ex-journalist was disgraced.

In the end he became, in Korchnoi's words, a 'one-legged dissident'. Spassky now lives in France although he still plays for the Soviet team and retains his citizenship.

It is a sad life and clear demonstration of Russia's almost oriental aversion to losing face to the strongest Western power. Would the same sweeping purges have occured in U.S. sport, if, say, a Russian basketball team had beaten the American side? It seems extremely unlikely; the key component, ideology, has given an extra edge in every East-West encounter to the Communists.

To understand Communist success on the sportsfield we have to look at the roots of this ideological X-factor. How has it take such a firm hold of Communist sportsmen? What are its weaknesses?

Ideological use of sport was most glaring during the Cold War years. Then both the USA and USSR (and its Iron Curtain allies) were anxious to win the 'battle for men's minds'. UNESCO noted in a 1952 report that 'the Olympic Games are now regarded by many as just a testing ground for two great political units'.

In the age of instant television communication, simple political messages could be conveyed to several millions of people. And in the eyes of the Kremlin's political propaganda controllers – the international section of the Central Committee – every event had equivalent politi-

Right:
A two-year-old Russian gymnast with modest aspirations!

section message. Thus, if a US athlete was forced into second or third place by Communist athletes, Soviet television commentators during the 1950s used to point out that America was correspondingly 'weak' or 'decadent'.

In the United States too there was intense rivalry, a need to 'show the Reds that they can't have their own way', as one US commentator put. All in all, sport became 'war without weapons' at a time when the nuclear balance made the prospect of real war unthinkable.

Yet this ideological bitterness did not begin with the Cold War. It was an inherent part of Communist sport strategy from the beginning. After the Russian revolution, for example, sport was seen as a way of advancing 'proletarian internationalism'. In plain English, this meant that Russia was prepared to play sport only with other Communist or workers clubs and not with 'bourgeois' Western states. Maxim Gorky, the Russian author, was particularly scathing about Western sport: 'Bourgeois sport has one principal purpose – to make men even more stupid than they are'. By contrast Communist sport was intended to enlighten men and make them more critical of the ruling class.

In international terms, the Communists used sport to seal links with foreign workers' movements rather than truly pit their skills against Western competition. Soccer was the main tool

in this: it did not need much equipment and was easily organised around local factory clubs. The first ever international soccer match played in the Soviet Union was against the Finnish workers' team in 1922. The Moscow team won 7-1. During the 1920s such matches increased rapidly with Russian sides doing well against French Communists and against the Polish, Norwegian and German workers' associations.

Things began to change in the mid-1920s, because of the vast political turmoil. The power struggle between Trotsky, who believed in 'exporting' revolution, and Stalin, who wanted to consolidate socialism in one country, finally resolved itself in favor of Stalin. This forced a more national character on Soviet sport. It was not intended to unify the nation and would act internationally only as a prestige symbol. This meant, in short, that Russia decided only to enter those tournaments in which it was almost certain to win a large number of events.

On the battlefield or sportsfield, Stalin was above all concerned with avoiding defeat. This pushed him into a surprising alliance with Hitler after the Munich agreement of 1938 showed him that the West were not suitable allies. He was convinced that Hitler intended to attack Russia and he decided that there were only two alternatives: either to secure a guarantee of Russian neutrality in a future war between Germany and

Left:
Kornelia Ender, East German swimming superstar.

Above:
World Table Tennis championship finals tend to be all-Chinese affairs. But in 1977 China's Kuo Yao-Hua lost to Kohno of Japan.

the West, or to make an actual alliance with Na[zi] Germany and thus buy time. In the end t[he] Molotov-Ribbentrop non-aggression pa[ct] between Russia and Germany, gave Stalin t[he] breathing space he wanted and an appare[nt] guarantee of immunity from attack.

So Communist sport was set for anoth[er] ideological head-over-heels. The first ev[er] sports agreement signed between the Sov[iet] Union and the West was with Nazi Germa[ny] which should logically have been the arc[h] enemy of the Soviet Union.

Under the German-Soviet sports agreeme[nt] Russian gymnasts, swimmers and weightlifte[rs] competed in Germany while German fence[rs,] swimmers, soccer players, athletes and ten[nis] players visited the Soviet Union. More spo[rts] contests were organised between German a[nd] Russian sportsmen during 1940 than betwe[en] the USSR and the rest of the world in all of t[he] years since the 1917 revolution. This connecti[on] with German sport – which gave Russia its fi[rst] real taste of international competition has last[ed] until the present day. Although the Soviet Uni[on] has given East Germany the ideologi[cal] framework for its sports machine, Soviet o[ffi]cials made clear to the authors that they ha[ve] learned much from the East Berlin sports lea[d]ership.

All-round skating champion Boris Stenin feted on his return to Russia in 1960.

48

g Blokhin of Russia
ving against Canada
he 1976 Olympics.

ow:
y v. Russia: a soccer
endly' at the Lenin
dium in Moscow,
5.

The invasion of Russia by Hitler ended all contacts with Nazi sportsmen and indeed Moscow had no international sports links between 1941 and 1945. Almost all young men were called up while most young women took their places in factories and on the farms.

In many ways this hit Russia's confidence in the sporting field and the first instinct of the sporting authorities after the war was to suspend competition with the West for a decade. The natural reserve of athletes had been decimated by the war and there seemed no immediate chance of recovery.

But Stalin overruled these doubts and insisted that the USSR show the West that it was stronger than ever on the sporting field. 'Each new victory,' said a Communist party resolution in 1949, 'is a victory for the Soviet form of society and the socialist system.'

Interestingly enough, Russia and the other Iron Curtain countries used soccer as the initial way of breaking into international sport again. The USSR had done much the same after the 1917 revolution: soccer was the one sport in which the Eastern Bloc felt confident enough to tackle the West with at this early stage.

The team selected for the Russian bre[ak] through was Moscow Dynamo. Only two mor[e] after the war, the Dynamo soccer team accep[ted] invitations to visit Sweden, Norway and Brit[ain] and, as (the writer and journalist) George Orw[ell] recorded, the effect was shattering.

At a time when Britain was considered to [be] the supreme soccer playing nation, Dyna[mo] beat Cardiff 10-1, Arsenal 4-3 and drew v[ith] Chelsea 3-3 and Glasgow Rangers 2-2. S[port] had again served its purpose: it showed [the] West that Russia was still strong, despite the l[oss] of 20 million people in the war.

With this auspicious start, soccer was see[n as] a natural instrument by the other East Europ[ean] countries to break into the international sp[ort] though their results were less stunning t[han] Dynamo's. It is however, oversimplistic [to] assume that all the Communist states w[ere] mainly concerned with impressing the West [that] 'might was right.' Each country had its own po[int] to prove – although they used the same id[eo]logical tools to achieve their aim.

By 1949, 10 countries had adopted Soviet-ty[pe] systems and all, apart from China, w[ere] bequeathed the Soviet sports ideology. [The]

Safepour of Iran holds down Russia's Aliev in Greco-Roman wrestling bout in a classic setting: Rome, 1960.

other countries were Bulgaria, Yugoslavia, Albania, Hungary, Rumania, Poland, Czechoslovakia, North Korea and East Germany. Cuba too was to take over the Soviet sports philosophy.

That each country freely adapted the Soviet sports thinking to suit its own political purposes is clearly illustrated by East Germany, which used sport as one of the main ways of gaining international recognition. The official line in the 1950s was that reunification of Germany could only come about after East Germany, the so-called German Democratic Republic (GDR) was acknowledged to be the equal of West Germany. What better way to prove this than

through sport? Diplomatic means were more or less ruled out because the GDR was almost totally isolated – there were no Western ambassadors in East Berlin and no official visits from the West.

Sport was chosen as the means of breaching this blockade, symbolised by East Germany's struggle to be accepted as a separate state in the Olympic movement. The International Olympic Committee was initially only prepared to allow participation of a single all-German team made up of players from both Germanys. The GDR refused this solution and did not compete in the 1952 Games but accepted in time for the Melbourne Olympics four years later.

After solid campaigning by the East Germans – heavily backed, of course, by the Russians and other Iron Curtain countries – the IOC allowed the two Germanys to enter separate teams but only providing they used specially designed flags instead of their national flags. This was a particularly inconclusive move, stopping short of full recognition of the GDR. Only at the Munich Olympics in 1972 did the GDR achieve its aim of full recognition which was seen as a considerable ideological triumph for the Communist country, especially as it proved to have one of the strongest teams in the Games.

The amazing improvement in East Germany's sporting performance has certainly reinforced its political successes. In the 1950s West Germany was streaks ahead of the GDR in the Olympics medals table. Even in the Rome Olympics in 1960, West Germany won 10 gold medals against three by the GDR, 10 silver compared to nine by the East Germans. The big shift however, came between the Tokyo Games in 1964 and the Mexico Olympics.

	Gold		Silver		Bronze	
	West Ger.	GDR	West Ger.	GDR	West Ger.	GDR
Tokyo (1964)	7	3	15	7	12	6
Mexico (1968)	5	9	11	9	10	7

What was the reason for this dramatic improvement? Yet again ideological campaigning played its part. After the initially disappointing results, Soviet trainers and propaganda experts came to East Germany to explain to the younger generation that it was imperative to overtake West Germany, to show that the GDR was ideologically stronger. In the USSR, Krushchev (Stalin's successor) had already told his people that they must overtake the USA in economic, political and sporting terms by 1960. Now a similar message was conveyed by East German Communist Party Chief, Walter Ulbricht.

The new political drive had quite a few practical consequences: facilities were improved for the mass of sports enthusiasts and there was a purge of medium-ranking sports officials. But above all the shift was a psychological one.

Right:
Valeri Borzhov, Russi
great sprinter, at
Munich.

Below:
Aragats Sports Club:
the ladies shoot with
precision.

Leading sports bureaucrat Rudi Reichert told trainers and coaches that East Germany should use Moscow as a model of sporting performance instead of looking jealously at the USA. The Communist slogan became: 'Learn to be victorious – learn from the Soviet Union.'

Marxist ideology then can be adapted easily to meet national sporting goals. If the aim is international recognition or political superiority, then Communist ideology can adjust elastically to provide the necessary slogans and brainwashing. In describing sport before the Communist takeover, Fidel Castro, the Cuban leader, said it was intended only 'to provide entertainment for the children of rich families in their aristocratic schools and clubs . . . sport has been turned into a form of business, an object of exploitation'. This was not completely true – and Castro knew it. But he used sport in this way to turn the workers against the middle and mercantile classes and ultimately Cuban sport became a way of showing defiance towards the USA.

Under-pinning all these different functions of ideology, there is the idea that sport can be used to completely transform the belief of the population. Thus Krushchev saw sport as a means towards creating the 'New Socialist Man', all round servant of the state and the Communist party. Castro has elaborated on the idea: 'At the Olympics it was shameful to see the position occupied by Cuba because the rich, accustomed to good living, had not got the necessary spirit of sacrifice to be good athletes. Good athletes must come from the people, from the workers, because they are capable of sacrifice: they can be consistent and hardy.'

It is this spirit of sacrifice which Communist sport tries to foster. In practice this often means a concentration on team games over the more individual games like tennis. However, even in individualist games a kind of 'team' mentality prevails. Thus before major chess tournaments, the Soviet players often go through a strenuous course of joint fitness exercises and can be seen jogging through the countryside in the blue USSR tracksuits. By contrast US players often do not meet at all before a tournament and train individually.

Chess provides an interesting example of how the 'spirit of sacrifice' can really work for Communist sportsmen. Korchnoi, somewhat shamefacedly tells the story of how he originally won his initial Masters title, the first rung of the international ladder. To secure his Masters 'norm' he had to win a match against a fellow Russian player (this was of course long before Korchnoi defected) who was considerably

older than Korchnoi. At the crucial match, pressure was put on the older player to throw the game: chess and Party officials told him that he should lose for the sake of Soviet chess and allow Korchnoi's young talent to bloom. Korchnoi, they argued, was full of promise and a defeat could spoil him for the future service of the Soviet Union. The rival, a well-established player, gave way, made a deliberate mistake and Korchnoi won.

Korchnoi has since proved many times that he would have won the Masters title at some stage without effort. But it was an illustration of how tough the ideological pressures can be. The aim is to breed a New Soviet Man; ideally a young, well educated, modest man from the working classes who can provide inspiration for the masses. Anything that stands in the way of that aim is swept aside. Korchnoi was once the beneficiary of that. Now, ironically, Korchnoi's bug-bear, Anatoly Karpov, is the blue-eyed model of Communist sporting philosophy: a graphic reminder that what counts behind the Iron Curtain is the system not the individual.

4 Triumphs and Defeats

Living standards in the Communist world, in Eastern Europe, China and Cuba, have risen dramatically since the Second World War. The advances have been impressive as governments have steered their people through the misery of revolution, war and lives that were in many cases still feudal into the 20th century. Despite this progress life for the Communist masses remains, certainly by Western standards, hard and austere. In Eastern Europe however, and in the Soviet Union in particular, an elaborate but shadowy system of privilege has evolved to ensure that life for some is not only comfortable but actually luxurious. It guarantees a fortunate elite the luxuries denied the majority: smart clothes, fine food, well-furnished town houses and quiet country retreats, cars and foreign travel.

Members of this elite, probably about two million strong in the Soviet Union alone, do not necessarily earn more than their comrades working in factories or on farm collectives. But then money in Communist society matters less than status, position and influence. In the early seventies, for example, Soviet President Leonid Brezhnev was earning less than a senior government administrator. Yet in real terms his life was incomparably more comfortable: chauffeur driven limousines on 24-hour call, a string of well equipped town and country homes, the finest food and clothes and a travelling cortege of private doctors. Of course Brezhnev stood at the apex of the pyramid of privilege. But even the lowliest member of this new aristocracy can expect a lifestyle that bears no resemblance to that endured by the masses.

The general outline may be clear but it is more difficult – since governments deny that privilege exists under Communism – to discover the mechanics of recruitment to the elite. From the reports of Western journalists working in Eastern Europe it would seem that there are two main criteria governing recruitment: political orthodoxy and usefulness to the state. Party members, administrators, doctors, scientists, writers, artists, journalists, academics, senior army officers and security agents – all can expect to be admitted to the ranks of the privileged. And given the importance of sport in the Communist propaganda war it is hardly surprising that sportsmen and sportswomen are also found there. Sport, after all, is a key weapon with which to flay the West and show that Communism really is superior. The stars, the men and women who take the medals and honors at the showpiece international events, are the new gladiators of Socialism, rewarded with titles (Merited Master of Sport of the USSR, Master of Sport, International Class) as well as with cars, homes and clothes.

Discussion of such blatant elitism – a contradiction of everything that Communism is meant to stand for – is predictably and effectively stifled by the security forces and the censorship machine. But evidence of all-pervasive corruption cannot be hidden from whole populations and every young Russian, East German or Czech knows full well that there are ways to escape the drudgery of ordinary life. What are their options?

They can hope to join the Party, serve loyally and scale the bureaucratic ladder onto the first rung of the elite. They can study for careers in medicine, journalism, science or the arts and hope for recognition. Such routes though are long and arduous. Children and humble factory or farm workers are rarely given the chance to attend good enough schools to even consider such exalted professions. And children of better-off parents know that talent in such desirable professions often counts less than the most mind-numbing and unbending political orthodoxy. One slip of the tongue as they worked their way towards the elite would spell ruin. Many youngsters therefore choose sport as the safest, surest route to the good life. In sport, they reason correctly, more than any other elite career talent is marginally, but significantly, more valued by the state than ideological commitment.

The motivation to find a way to a life of privilege is markedly more powerful for these East Europeans than the attraction to make a million is for a Western youngster. Since the war the Communist governments, especially in East Germany and the Soviet Union, have maintained that the arms and heavy industries must take precedence over the production of consumer goods. As a result of this policy – that the citizen should produce rather than consume – the average worker faces acute shortages in consumer products that are widely available in the West.

Right:
To the Chinese, defea at table tennis is no laughing matter.

Left:
A riot during a soccer match between El Salvador and Russia.

Curtains hide the occupants of a limousine driving dow the special fast lane in Moscow reserved for Russia's elite.

58

Food supplies are spasmodic and unpredictable. Meat for example, disappears for months on end without explanation or excuse from the authorities. Cars are so expensive that it takes years to save for one and even then delivery is often delayed for many months. Housing is generally poor and furniture difficult to obtain. There are queues everywhere and for everything – theater tickets, sports events, rail tickets. everything, it seems, is in short supply. Foreign travel is too impossibly expensive to even contemplate. Even travel within the state or to other parts of the Communist world is difficult.

For elite athletes life is rather more relaxed. Paid by the state to train, compete and of course win, they clearly enjoy the fruits of success. The most treasured privilege of all is the freedom to travel to the West, a right granted to only a handful even amongst the elite and that after thorough vetting by the security forces. Travel to the West is not only valued for the excitement and glamour it offers. There are very tangible material benefits too.

With just one careful shopping trip to London or New York an athlete can easily double his annual income. It is not strange therefore that most touring Communist athletes show more interest in Western shops than historic monuments or museums when they are free of training and competition. they all know that cameras, radios, watches, books, records and clothes, particularly denim jeans, will fetch astronomic prices on the black market at home. But importing Western goods is only one aspect of this lucrative business. Professional East European athletes, like tennis players, can also import foreign currency. It can be exchanged at ten to fifteen times its face value for the domestic Communist currency on the black market or spent in hotels or restaurants – which provide the only worthwhile nightlife in Communist cities – where only hard foreign currency is accepted. And athletes who are astute enough to save their dollars, pounds or deutschmarks in the months between trips to the West know that they will have no trouble disposing of them at the well stocked foreign currency shops that dot major Communist cities.

Even forgetting the profits that are made from foreign trips elite athletes still enjoy an inestimably higher standard of living than the masses. As members of the privileged class they can shop throughout the year at special stores set aside for the elite. The authorities deny the existence of these 'super stores' – as they deny all inconvenient and embarrassing facts – but they are perhaps the best known and most resented perks of the entire, complex system of privilege.

The authorities can never keep their location a secret, no matter how anonymous a building they choose, because every 'super-store' is signposted by the lines of large cars parked outside, the chauffeurs idly puffing on cigarettes whilst their masters and mistresses stock up with goods that are rarely seen on the open market.

The ordinary workers often find themselves facing other irritating, if less concrete, proof that elitism thrives in their midst. Workers frequently find that reservations for seats at the opera or ballet have somehow been mislaid. Safely instaled on an inter-state flight they find that they are asked to leave because of a 'booking error'. There is no recourse. Everyone knows what has happened: a member of the elite, perhaps a football player or swimmer, has demanded a place or a seat and the booking clerk has simply complied with the demand by ousting the humble worker.

Athletes even have advantages over fellow members of the elite. The ranking system – a pyramid of titles awarded on the basis of training and competition – provides athletes with both guidelines and security. Writers or artists are always unsure of where they stand in the hierarchy of privilege and can only speculate on exactly what perks they can demand without offending their masters. Athletes have an idea at least merely by remembering their ranking: Masters of Sport know, for instance, that they will be able safely to request more privileges

than the lower ranking Candidate Masters of Sport. Athletes have greater security too once established within the elite. A painting that is considered a little avant garde or a book that contains one or two controversial passages can ruin the career of an artist or writer. An athlete is rarely punished after a run of poor performances – though, of course, continued failure would inevitably be penalised.

This is not to say that athletes do not have to respect certain conventions imposed by the authorities. A written code demands that ranked athletes 'conduct themselves in accordance with the Moral Code of the Builder of Communism and the code of sporting ethics'; that they 'constantly improve their skills, political and social and physical'; that they 'are members of sports collectives'; that they 'observe a sporting regime, good health standards and are constantly under medical supervision' and that they 'take part in the sports movement and pass on their expertise to others'. The unwritten code demands that athletes should not abuse the substantial privileges they are granted. Occasionally a newspaper in Eastern Europe carries a paragraph or two, usually after the offence in question, hinting at the fate that befalls athletes if they are unwise enough to take the authorities for a ride.

In 1972 the Soviet press said that some athletes had been found guilty of selling the badges awarded for sporting excellence: a Merited Master of Sport badge had been fetch-

Left:
The wedding of Russia's favorite children, world gymnastics champion Lyudmila Turishcheva and twice Olympic gold medallist Valeri Borzhov was a more dignified affair.

Right:
Ilie Nastase's wedding receives Western-style celebrity treatment.

35 roubles and a Master of sport badge 20 ...ubles. The seventies have also seen growing ...idence of widespread abuse of privilege – in ...me cases criminal corruption – in major ...orts. Football particularly has been affected, ...inly because of the amounts of cash gener-...ed by the game. In 1971 the newspaper *Kom-...mol' skaya pravda* revealed that a top soccer

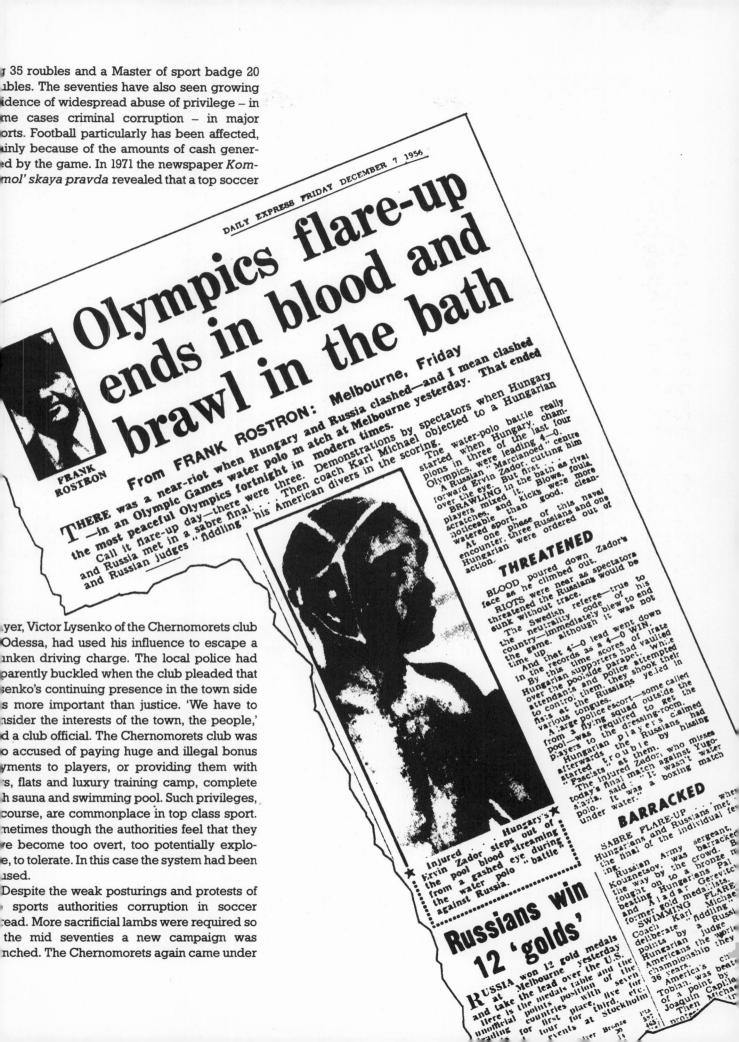

DAILY EXPRESS FRIDAY DECEMBER 7 1956

Olympics flare-up and ends in blood and brawl in the bath

FRANK ROSTRON

From FRANK ROSTRON: Melbourne, Friday

THERE was a near-riot when Hungary and Russia clashed—and I mean clashed —in an Olympic Games water polo match at Melbourne yesterday. That ended the most peaceful Olympics fortnight in modern times.

Call it flare-up day—there were three. Demonstrations by spectators when Hungary and Russia met in a sabre final. Then coach Karl Michael objected to a Hungarian and Russian judges "fiddling" his American divers in the scoring.

The water-polo battle really started when Hungary, cham-pions in three of the last four Olympics, were leading 4—0.

A Russian "Marcianoed" centre forward Ervin Zador, cutting him over the eye. But first

BRAWLING in the bath as rival players mixed it. Blows, fouls, scratches, and kicks were more noticeable than good, clean-watered sport.

At one phase of this naval encounter, three Russians and one Hungarian were ordered out of action.

THREATENED

BLOOD poured down Zador's face as he climbed out.

RIOTS were near as spectators threatened the Russians would be sunk without trace.

The Swedish referee—true to the neutrality code of his country—immediately blew to end the game, although it was not time up.

And that 4—0 lead went down in the records as a 4—0 WIN.

By this time scores of irate Hungarian supporters had vaulted over the poolside parapet. White attendants and police attempted to control them, they shook their fis:s at the Russians yelled in various tongues.

A large police escort—some called from a flying squad outside the pool—was required to get the Hungarian players to the dressing-room.

Players claimed afterwards the Russians had started trouble by hissing "Fascists" at them.

The injured Zador, who missed today's final match against Yugo-slavia, said: It wasn't water polo. It was a boxing match under water."

BARRACKED

SABRE FLARE-UP: when Hungarians and Russians met in the final of the individual fe...ing.

Russian Army sergeant, Kouznetsov, was barracked all the way by the crowd. B... fought on to a bronze m... beating Hungarians Pal... and Aladar Gerevitc... former gold medalists.

SWIMMING FLARE... Coach Karl Michae... deliberate "fiddling" points by a Russi... Hungarian the worl... Americans they...

championship 36 years. America's c... Tobian was beat... of a point by beat... of Joaquin Capilla...

Then protes...

Injured Hungary's Ervin Zador steps out of the pool blood streaming from a gashed eye during the water polo "battle" against Russia.

Russians win 12 'golds'

RUSSIA won 12 gold medals at Melbourne yesterday and take the lead over the U.S. Here is the medals table and the unofficial points position with first place for ...urth events etc., five for second, third ... place, with four for ... countries ... at Stockholm ...

...yer, Victor Lysenko of the Chernomorets club ...Odessa, had used his influence to escape a ...unken driving charge. The local police had ...parently buckled when the club pleaded that ...senko's continuing presence in the town side ...s more important than justice. 'We have to ...nsider the interests of the town, the people,' ...d a club official. The Chernomorets club was ...o accused of paying huge and illegal bonus ...yments to players, or providing them with ...s, flats and luxury training camp, complete ...h sauna and swimming pool. Such privileges, ...course, are commonplace in top class sport. ...metimes though the authorities feel that they ...ve become too overt, too potentially explo-...e, to tolerate. In this case the system had been ...used.

...Despite the weak posturings and protests of ...sports authorities corruption in soccer ...ead. More sacrificial lambs were required so ...the mid seventies a new campaign was ...nched. The Chernomorets again came under attack for 'handing out all sorts of bonuses and payments'. Moscow Dynamo striker Anatoly Shepel was suspended and labeled an unprincipled moneygrabber for selling the Volvos he was given by the government, The pattern is always identical: select an athlete or a sports club and make an example of them to serve as a warning to others. Such a policy also gives the impression to the masses that the regime is unaware of and unwilling to tolerate privilege.

Athletes who are violent on the field or in the arena are less of an embarrassment than those who break the rules in other ways. Bad behavior by sportsmen, believe the authorities, is rephrehensible but hardly constitutes a threat to the system. And violence, especially in football and ice hockey, has been increasing in the past decade. Press coverage of violent incidents remains, however, sparse and highly selective; a controlled trickle rather than an objective flow of information. the few reports that do filter through to the West show that the careers of athletes who become involved in fights or arguments with referees and judges are rarely permanently damaged. In 1971, for example, the football match between Rostov and Neftchi degenerated into an open brawl. Banischevsky, the international who had supposedly been banned for his part in an earlier brawl, tried to lead his players off the field in an effort to calm the situation – and was swiftly attacked for adding to the problems of the referee. The Soviet press seized on the match as an indication of a trend that was threatening to ruin soccer. 'Victory at all costs', said the papers, was not the right attitude for Soviet sportsmen, 'It is perverting sport and is contrary to Soviet ethics'. Moreover it was teaching young people 'bad habits' and presenting a harmful image to the world. There were demands for life bans on the players involved. All this was hypocritical nonsense: Soviet athletes are amongst the most success-

World champion weightlifter Vasili Alexeyev at work as a miner.

sessed in Eastern Europe, taught from child-
od that winning is vital to the well being of the
te. The storm soon died and none of the
stov or Neftchi players suffered for their
havior. Violent conduct, as far as Western
rnalists know, is generally punished in this
y – by an outcry and a painless rap over the
uckles.

Of course the majority of athletes talented
ough to be selected for international competi-
n or top teams are too sensible to endanger
eir place in the elite by indiscretions. This
alty is rewarded by the state when they
entually retire. Taking boxers as an example –
group hardly noted for their achievements
tside the ring – it is clear that the state ensures
t elite athletes remain comfortable when the
ys of glory are over. Former Soviet champion
nstantin Gradpol became, of all things, a uni-
rsity professor. Another, Boris Lagutin, be-
me a lawyer and a third, Gennady Shatkov,
came rector of the prestigious Leningrad
iversity. Former world gymnast champion
dmilla Turishcheva, always a paragon of
cialist virtue, became a coach and teacher
d apparently wrote a thesis on 'The Effects of
e Performance Emotional Tension in Gym-
stics on Competitive Performance'. It is a simi-
story in East Germany, the second most suc-
ssful Communist country and one whose
orts system most closely resembles that of the
SR. Ex-champion athletes Ulla Donath,
nfred Matuschewski and Renate Dannhauer
ve all been given plum jobs in the sports
chine.

In China, however, the government seems to
be trying to avoid creating such a privileged
elite. It was only in the mid seventies, after the
internal seizures that followed the rule of
Madame Mao and her Gang of Four, that China
began to open her door to Western journalists
and knowledge of that vast country, which
includes one quarter of the world's population, is
still fragmented and incomplete. Whilst in many
respects the Chinese sports system was originally modeled on the Soviet system – when relations between the two countries were close –
there are mounting differences. Potential world
class athletes are creamed off into elite schools
but cannot expect anything like the material
rewards of their counterparts in Eastern Europe.

As they progress towards international class
their feet are kept firmly planted on the ideological ground: they have to tour China lecturing
to peasants and their studies, of Mao, the role of
sport under Communism, are taken more
seriously than in other Communist states. With
China gradually re-entering international
competition, having rejected the rigid anti-
competitive philosophy of the Gang of Four,
sport will naturally begin to assume a greater
importance in its society. And as athletes too
grow in stature it is possible that the material
rewards awaiting successful competitors will
increase. For the moment those rewards are
small.

Olga Korbut was a 17 year old schoolgirl, 4
feet 11 inches tall and weighing just under six
stones, when she arrived in Munich for the '72
Olympic Games as an unknown member of the
Soviet gymnastics squad. When she left, having
won two individual gold medals, one silver and

Left:
*Opposite ends of the
scale: diminutive Olga
Korbut and
not-so-diminutive
weightlifting champ
Vasili Alexeyev, close
friends, returning from
Munich.*

Right:
*The ping-pong
diplomats: Chinese
table tennis officials
welcome American
visitors
in 1972.*

63

one team gold, she had become an international celebrity. She had appeared on television for no more than 30 minutes in all but the audience had run into hundreds of millions and the impact had been immediate and astonishing. The sports writers vied with each other to produce the most colorful profile. Newspapers dropped adjectives and superlatives like confetti on to breakfast tables: Olga was 'enchanting', a 'pig-tailed elfin', 'a beguiling genius'. They argued that it was her humanity as much as her talent on the beams and bars that made her so exceptional. It was a rare chance for the journalists, after years of success by anonymous and unsmiling East Europeans, and they certainly did not falter for a moment. The public, shocked by the massacre of Israeli athletes by Palestinian terrorists, were only too ready to fall in love with Korbut; she seemed to embody the innocence that had been so sadly missing from the Games.

To be fair Korbut did have charm as well as ability. She wept, smiled and wept again with equal emotion. She was a natural showman well as a natural athlete – rather like boxin Muhammed Ali, tennis' Ille Nastase or athleti Steve Ovett. Like them she reveled in the ma event and in the involvement and adoration o crowd. Korbut's success may have surprised t sportswriters but it had been anticipated Western experts on Eastern Europe. They kne that children were being selected at ever earl ages for training at elite schools. It had or been a matter of time before someone like Ko but – the first of the child prodigies – emerge And their fears about the possible harmful si effects – both mental and physical – of subje ing children to such relentless training a competition were borne out by the developme of Korbut after Munich.

Her early career followed the usual cou for any precociously talented Soviet youngst She was born on May 16, 1955 in the small ind trial town of Grodno, 300 miles West of Mosco on the Polish border. Her father Valentin wa

Right:
Emotion shows on the face of Olga Korbut; the world's darling in Munich four years earlier, she has just been 'dethroned' by Rumania's Nadia Comaneci at Montreal and, at 17 already seems to be over the hill.

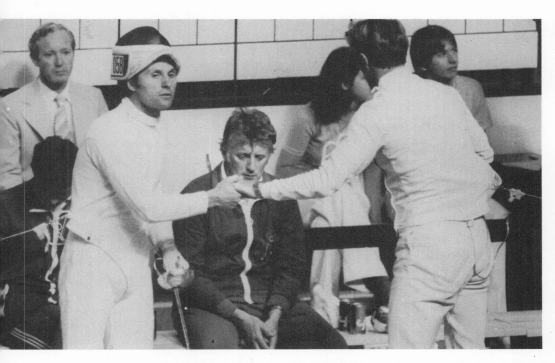

Left:
see page 66.

Below left:
The strain of disappointment: Rumania's Valerie Stefanescu in tears after failing to qualify for the 100 m hurdles final in Montreal.

Below right:
Leonid Zhabotinsky, Russian champion weightlifter of the mid-sixties, makes a rare mistake.

Top:
Boris Onischenko, the Russian pentathlete, has his epée examined before being disqualified for cheating in the fencing event at Montreal, 1976. The Soviet drive for success pushed him too far. Picture on page 65 shows Onischenko shaking hands with his British opponent, Jim Fox immediately before the incident.

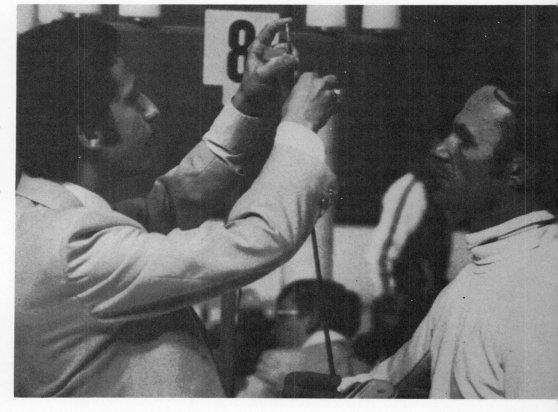

Below:
Natalya Yurchenko, the new Russian gymnastic 'Wunderkind' being prepared for the 1980 Olympics under the watchful eye of the senior team coach.

Training sessions at a children's Olympic preparatory school in Leningrad.

retired engineer and, significantly, a former nationalist patriot in the war against the Germans. There is no doubt that having a father with such dubious ideological past – nationalists were counter-revolutionaries – was filed away by the KGB (for future reference) when Korbut was earmarked for training at an elite school. After being spotted by coaches from the town's special sports school – one of 35 in the USSR with a gymnastics section – she began serious training. She was not yet 10 years old.

For the next eight years she was coached by Tokyo gold medallist Yelena Volchetsaya and National Champion Tamara Alexeyeva. 'At times she can be a little headstrong' they complained. For lesser athletes such criticism usually meant instant dismissal but Korbut was too obviously a potential Olympic champion for this to happen. Their faith was justified when she later became the youngest ever 'Master of Sports' in gymnastics. Once again however her outspokeness had been noticed by the security forces: during the 1970 World Championships in Yugoslavia as a reserve for the Soviet squad she complained to the judges that she had been passed over because of internal jealousies in the team.

After Munich Korbut retired for two months to a secluded Soviet spa. Western journalists were told she was merely tired but there were fears that her exhaustive training – up to eight hours a day – and her uniquely adventurous routines were taking their toll. Meanwhile the International Gymnastics Federation discussed banning some exercises because they were too dangerous – discussions prompted by Korbut's displays at Munich. Her reaction was once again an embarrassment to the Soviets: 'If the ban is implemented then I see no future for me in gymnastics. It has always been the right of gymnasts to determine their own style'.

A year later – during the tour of the United States and Britain – the Soviet administration began to have doubts about the extraordinary personality cult that was growing up around Korbut. Officially sportswriters – who always echo the views of the Soviet establishment – were delighted with her popularity. In articles written for consumption in the West they alternated between quoting the American and British press on Korbut and explaining that Soviet athletes were only part of the great Socialist sports movement. And clearly the tour did present new and unwelcome problems for the Soviets. Korbut was mobbed in all eight of the American cities that the team visited. Chicago – included in the schedule after a personal plea from the city's Mayor Daley – declared March 26th, 1973 'Olga Korbut Day'.

The American press amply reflected the hysteria of the audiences. 'She stands elfin . . . cute in the wings . . . Olga, Olga, chant some of her pre-teenage fans and she flashes thanks with her pony tail to pony tail smile . . . Suddenly the cue. Olga the Personable becomes Olga the Intense. She dances into the spotlight and the evening becomes electric,' raved the *Christian Science Monitor*. The *Philadelphia Inquirer* went even further saying that the history of gymnastics could be divided into two phases: 'BO and AO, Before Olga and After Olga.' There was a boom in the sport in the States and Britain – entirely due, said the press, to Korbut. Letters, many addressed to 'Olga, Moscow', poured into the Soviet Union.

By now the Soviet machine was in total disarray. Before Korbut's Munich performance the Soviet press had controled the degree of hero worship accorded athletes. Too much was dangerous, lifting the athlete beyond the control of the state, rather as had happened in the case of the writer Solzhenitsyn. Too little meant that the masses had no idols – and that meant interest in sport diminished. This confusion and mounting hostility was reflected by the comments of Korbut's coaches and team mates. Only Renald Knysh, who had taught Olga from her days of a novice, tried to defend her. Her popularity could not, he said, be explained in terms of 'gymnastic superiority' but only by her natural innocence. She was, he added, very 'taken aback and embarrassed.' From Ludmilla Turishcheva, the elder stateswomen of Soviet gymnastics, there was only a stony silence. Two years later (in 1975) the hostility that had always existed between the two became public knowledge when a Western journalist asked Turishcheva if she would pose for a photograph with Korbut. 'I have no objection but I don't think that Olga will want to,' she said. Sure enough, Korbut said that she was too busy. Unlike Korbut, a girl overwhelmed by sudden fame, Turishcheva had never forgotten the ground rules that governed the behavior of elite athletes. She had shunned the flashy individualism that Korbut loved and was rewarded with cars, a flat, clothes, records – and of course a lucrative job when she retired.

Even after Munich Korbut was still living relatively modestly – as if the state couldn't quite decide whether or not to include her in the ranks of the privileged elite. By now she had no friends. One coach said of her: 'She has the temperament of an opera singer. She can be a bitch sometimes.' Ludmilla Turishcheva said: 'Perhaps she has other things on her mind than just sport.' Nemisis for Korbut came, ironically if predictably, in the shape of another child star –

Left:
Kornelia Ender wears her Montreal medal tally.

Below:
East German swimm stars Kornelia Ender and fiancé Roland Matthes.

Left:
A contemplative Turishcheva.

Right:
Nadia Comaneci.

dia Comaneci. As the 14 year old Rumanian
ept aside the challenge of the Soviets at the
ntreal Olympics – with routines that reached
ew level of excellence – Korbut faded from
scene.

Aged 21, with black shadows around her
es and lines that touched the corners of her
uth, she knew that her future had depended
another medal winning performance. Less
n a year later she announced her retirement
h typical defiance: 'It is not for me to hold fifth
sixth spot in the team.' A year later, as if to
phasise that she had never been part of the
rts machine, she married pop singer Leonid
tkevich. Pictured in the Western press in
9 after the birth of a son she seemed to have
d beyond her years.

Four months later she again featured in the
stern press: 'Olga Korbut, the darling of

*Rumanian gymnastics
queen Nadia Comaneci
sitting on the sidelines
during a West Germany
v. Rumania competition.
Unfit and overweight,
her spell in the limelight
seemed over.*

Below:
*Russia won gold and
silver medals in the
500 m ice speed skating
event at the 1956 Winter
Games at Cortina.*

ofilo Stevenson of
ba, the new Ali,
poses of his
manian co-finalist in
ntreal.

ow Left:
dmila Pakhornova
d Alexandra
rshkov, ice dance
ampions at
sbruck's Winter
ympics in 1976.

ow:
at professional sport
n bring: two great
xing champions, Ali
d Frazier, slug it out
glory and millions of
llars during their
ssic first fight, March
71.

gymnastics, is in training again and hoping to qualify for the Russian team at the 1980 Moscow Olympics. Can she do it' wrote one British newspaper. Korbut admitted that the training 'hurt' but added: 'I am determined to try and get back to my former standard. I'm hoping that I won't be just as good as I used to be. I want to be better.' She claimed that she had felt compeled to return to gymnastics because 'the present competitors are very good technically but don't have any soul'.

There have been suggestions – probably unjustified in this case – that Korbut was the victim of puberty retarding drugs, used, it was said, in Eastern Europe by gymnastics coaches to prevent awkward bulges developing on girl stars. It is clear though she had paid dearly for those years of training and competition and that unlike many other athletes had never been substantially rewarded. It seems as if the system has

rejected the first of its child stars and any hopes of a comeback, a second chance were always destined to fail.

Comaneci has fared better. The response to her Montreal display – three gold medals, one team silver and one individual bronze – was more subdued than that which had greeted Korbut four years earlier. The world now wondered whether it was desirable to take young girls – Comaneci was five when she began serious training – and subject them to such intense mental and physical pressures. After Montreal Comaneci – spared the spotlight of publicity endured by Korbut and living in the more relaxed atmosphere of Rumania – seemed to have managed the difficult transition from child star to mature athlete. She was allowed to develop physically – she put on several stones within months of the Olympics – despite the problems this presented for her beam and bar routines. There was no evidence that her trainers even tried to slow down this maturing by drugs or starvation diets. A year before the 1980 Moscow Olympics she announced that she would retire after the Games – recognising no doubt that well built young women had little chance in the age of the pencil slim child gymnasts. A combination of circumstances – a more mature temperament, less publicity, a more benevolent government – saved her from the fate that awaited Korbut. The next child wonder may perhaps not be so fortunate.

Boris Onischenko was, like Korbut, a casualty of the Communist system. But he paid a higher price for the Soviet philosophy that taking part was of no value unless you won. Onischenko, nominally a Red Army Major but in reality a full-time athlete and sports instructor, arrived in Montreal as one of the leading pentathletes in the world. He had been a key member of the Soviet squad for over a decade and had had a dazzling career: a gold medallist in the '69, '73 and '74 World Championships and a silver medallist at the Munich Games in 1972. In the Soviet Union he was already a respected member of the sports hierarchy; the epitome of the Socialist Man and held up as an example of how sport could mould character.

He was 38 when he stepped into the arena to meet Britain's Jim Fox in the epée fencing section of the pentathlon. As Fox said: 'He seemed very cheerful. He had been telling everyone that he expected to be promoted to Lieutenant Colonel when he went home.' There was, or so it appeared, nothing left for Boris to provide. He was in the twilight of his career and could look forward to a prosperous retirement as a member of the elite. A few minutes later his life

Anatoly Karpov, world chess champion flexes his muscles against the next generation in the Leningrade Palace of Pioneers.

Below:
Russian gymnasts rehearsing in London for their assault on the west, following their great success in Munich. The photo shows Olga Korbut, the flashpoint of the world gymnastics explosion.

lay in ruins. The story of how 'Boris the Che[at] had rigged his epée – with an electrical circ[uit] to register non-existent hits – made front pa[ge] news throughout the West. At first the Sovi[ets] denied the allegations: it was Western pro[p]aganda, they said. After a few hours it beca[me] clear that Onishchenko had indeed cheated. [He] was disowned by his country, locked in his ro[om] and promptly escorted back to the Soviet Un[ion] in the company of two burly KGB guards.

His fellow athletes in the Olympic villa[ge] were stunned. Why would Onischenko r[isk] everything? As Fox said: 'God knows what w[ill] happen to him now . .' Another athlete sa[id:] 'There is so much pressure on the East Eu[ro]peans. So many pressures are put on co[m]petitors and the need to win is too great.' One c[an] only speculate on the reasons for Onischenk[o's] action – he was certain to be caught. After [so] many years of feeling that he had to win, or [at] least perform very well, it seems likely that [he] was unable to grasp that that no longer m[at]tered; that he had already won his place for l[ife] amongst the elite. Perhaps he felt the need [of] just one more title to guarantee that life [of] privilege.

Back in the Soviet Union, stripped of his h[on]ors and commission, he disappeared for seve[ral] months. He told one Western journalist that [he] was 'resting' and in November that year t[he] official Novosti press agency said the he mig[ht] be allowed back to competitive sport. A 'hum[an] element' remained, said the agency, and t[he] doors were not necessarily irrevocably shut[. It] was an empty statement. Onischenko has n[ot] been heard of since. One report said that he w[as] driving a taxi in Leningrad and another said th[at,] facing a life of disgrace and insults and ev[en] hardship, he had committed suicide.

Cuban heavyweight Teofilo Stevens[on,] Olympic gold medallist in Munich and Montre[al] is another athlete who has benefited materia[lly] from success in competition – and from havi[ng] the correct political views. Stevenson, 20 yea[rs] old at Munich, was hailed as a worthy success[or] to former champions – like Joe Frazier, Geor[ge] Foreman and Muhammed Ali. Four years aft[er] the '72 Games – having rejected countle[ss] multi-million dollar offers to fight Ali for t[he] world title – he arrived in Montreal as the fi[rst] Olympic gold medallist to defend his title. [By] that time he was already a national hero in Cub[a,] ranking only slightly behind the leader of t[he] revolution Fidel Castro. And his relaxed, car[e]free lifestyle reflected that status: training, a litt[le] study and public appearances.

His triumph at Montreal – the first heav[y]weight to retain the Olympic crown – conso[li]

ated his position. The government offered him
nd his family a new home. Stevenson thanked
em, drew up his own plans and within months
oved into a luxury four-bedroom house. He
as elected – or rather *given* a place by the
uthorities – to the National Assembly. There
ere rumors, which had first circulated in 1976,
at he might turn professional but the attrac-
ons of that for Stevenson were only minimal.
lthough he was not wealthy he lived comfort-
bly and was assured of a place in the ruling
lite as a respected champion of the Cuban
evolution.

The rewards then for Stevenson were, even
y East European standards, considerable, and
e adulation that was allowed to build up quite
xceptional. Although the Cuban sports system
losely resembles that in other Communist
ountries – elite schools, early selection and
overnment backing for athletes – there are
ifferences, in spirit and attitude, and these help
xplain Stevenson's position. First, the Cubans
ave more in common with the American neg-
oes than the dour Soviets. Secondly, the revolu-
on that swept away capitalism came in 1959 and
e memories and habits of those pre-
ommunist days – including a love of individual-

ism – are still fresh. And thirdly Castro has
always enjoyed adulation and has never
regarded it as the evil it is looked on by the East
European leaders. Given these factors – imper-
fect central controls and some personal freedom – it is not surprising that Stevenson chose to
remain in Cuba. 'I am happy with my friends and
music. I do not yearn to be a rich man,' he said.
Sportsmen under capitalism were, he added,
'pieces of merchandise' and boxing for him,
unlike for the Western professionals, would
never become 'a means to live'. He continued:
'the love of eight million Cubans is worth more
than a million dollars. I am not interested in
professionalism, only in revolution.'

By all accounts Stevenson is an intelligent and
pleasant young man. He probably believes in
the abstract ideals of the Castro revolution but
he must know, in his heart at least, that his lifestyle owes everything to boxing – just as
Muhammad Ali's lifestyle did. In effect he had
turned professional from the moment he
stepped into the ring at Munich and his comfortable existence in a country still struggling to
eradicate poverty is as much a contradiction of
the Communist ideal as that of any professional
athlete in the West.

*Former record-holder
and six times champion
of the USSR, Honored
Master of Sports
Mikhail Krivonosov
(second left) has a
secure career in
coaching.*

5 Financing Victory

Among the spectators at the exhibition of Soviet gymnastics at Wembley Stadium in 1978, there were seven men in blue serge suits, trying hard to look British. They were in fact officials of the KGB (Komitet Gosudarstveni Bezopastni), the soviet Security Police. Three of them were there – understandably, given the demonstrations outside the stadium – to guard the young girls in the team. But the remainder were actually sports coaches fully paid up by the KGB.

It is not often realised in the West that the KGB – usually associated with spying operations and crackdowns on dissidents – is the most powerful sponsor of sport in the Soviet Union, providing facilities, funds and training for thousands of world-beating athletes.

This is the way that the Soviet and East European sports machines most effectively disguise and blur the distinction between amateurs and professionals. As in many Western countries, sportsmen receive back-hand payments and bonuses, they are given time off from work, and they are treated as a privileged class. But in no Western country is the back-up system of state support so extensive as behind the Iron Curtain.

The state backing is chaneled through various outlets – through factories, through regional sports clubs, through 'voluntary' organisations. But funds for the top athletes come from two main sources – the KGB and the army.

The main tool of the KGB's sporting activities is the Dynamo sports club which acts as an umbrella organsiation for soccer players, for gymnasts like the former world champion, Ludmilla Turishcheva, for boxers, water-polo players and figure skaters. this is not to say that all the sportsmen in the club are KGB agents, but most of the coaches, trainers, managers and chaperones have an official KGB rank and some-

times can be seen walking along the streets of Moscow in the distinctive olive-green garb of the organisation's uniformed branch.

The connection between the security service and the Dynamo sports club is rarely stated openly in the Communist press, though most of the older generation know of the link. It is a connection which goes back to 1923 and the flourishing relationship explains much about how the sports system works in the Soviet Union and in the other East European countries, to which the system was exported.

Dynamo was originally set up for the staff of the KGB and the border troops to keep them fit and provide them with cheap leisure time facilities. But there was another reason: in 1923, the KGB (or Cheka as it was then known) was the most feared organisation in the country – and it had to stay like that if it was to be effective. The mystique of the service, the argument ran, would have been diluted if the agents had mixed with ordinary citizens in conventional sports clubs.

This reasoning became all the more relevant during the 1930s when the security service – which had the main task of carrying out the purges which killed and imprisoned millions – was made directly subordinate to Josef Stalin. The KGB's role has been curbed somewhat since those days but it has been allowed to keep its important sporting influence.

The Dynamo club has spread its wings considerably since the early days and it seems now to have been given the specific function of raising the country's sporting standards. A Soviet journal recently defined Dynamo's functions – notice that the KGB link is still a strong element. 'Dynamo's task is to make physical culture and sport an integral part of the lives of all employ-

ees of the MVD (the Interior Ministry) and KGB and of their families, to promote mass sport, to encourage military and service sports in accordance with the physical manual of the USSR armed forces, to train proficient sportsmen and to prepare members of the Soviet Union for labor and the defence of their country.

This evangelistic zeal seems to have paid off both in domestic and international competition. For instance, four Dynamo-sponsored teams have been in the top division of the Soviet soccer league since 1974. In 1973 and 1974, Dynamo teams won the league. From 1975 to 1976, Dynamo Kiev (by Western standards a fully professional side) was used as the Soviet national team in all international matches, including the Olympics. this met with heavy criticism from other leading Soviet soccer clubs: to take a regional team and play it as the national side for so long, stifled the ambitions of other players and put too much pressure on the Kiev players themselves. Dynamo Kiev's performance at home and abroad started to flag and the Soviet selection committee was forced to reshuffle the national side a little.

Mate Parlov of
Yugoslavia: one of the
few Iron Curtain
sportsmen to succeed
professionally without
quitting his country, he
was European and
world
light-heavyweight
boxing champion.

The Dynamo role is strong in all the oth
sports too. At the 1972 Summer Olympic
Dynamo members made up one third of the to
Soviet Olympic team and collected twice
many medals as other Russian sports cl
members. At the Moscow Olympics, the str
on Dynamo sportsmen and sportswomen will
even stronger – some experts believe that t
Soviet side might be as much as 50 per ce
Dynamo.

With this sort of success being chalked up
was inevitable that other East European cou
tries would follow suit. To some extent this is t
natural consequence of the Soviet involveme
in the setting up of the secret services in oth
Warsaw Pact countries. In East Germany, f
example, Soviet officials still hold key positio
in the country's security service, co-ordinatin
closely on all operations in third countries. A
major project undertaken by the KGB's sist
party the Staatssicherheitsdienst (Stasi) has
have the seal of approval from Moscow.

The sports club of the Stasi was set up in 19
soon after the security service itself was estab
lished and is headed by Dr. Erich Mielke,
member of the ruling Politburo and Minister f

te Security. No wonder then, with this top-
vel interest, that the German Dinamo club is
e most sought after sporting organisation in
st Germany. In 1974 – the latest available figure
t had 230,000 members, of whom about 90,000
re children.

The East German Dinamo has netted over 50
ld medals at the Olympics and other inter-
tional matches and it had particular success
th its women athletes. Karin Janz, the gymnast
ho won two golds, a silver and a bronze at the
nich Olympics was a member of Dinamo, as
s Monika Zehrt who won a gold in the 400
tres.

Other countries have pursued a similar sys-
m – Bulgaria and Yugoslavia for instance – and
ey too have called their clubs Dynamo or
namo. But some countries, including Rumania
d China, have been reluctant to over-burden
eir security apparatus with the problems of
ading a sports organisation. In these coun-
es, the army is seen as a more suitable spon-
: for sport. Military skills blend more naturally
th sports training and it is easier to justify the
penditure.

In the Soviet Union too the army plays a key

role in organising and paying for sport – it is
second only to Dynamo in turning out regular
winners at international matches. The origins of
army involvement in sport goes back even
further than that of the KGB. Even under the
Czars, sports and military training went hand-
in-hand.

Under the Communists, military participation
has taken two forms. The Central Sports Club of
the Red Army (TSKA) was established, like
Dynamo, in 1923 and fast became the main rival
of the KGB club. But like Dynamo, it was a semi-
elite organisation: entry into the club was highly
competitive for non-military sportsmen. A soldier who failed to meet regular test standards is
pushed down TSKA's team structure until it
becomes clear to the unfortunate athlete that he
is no longer wanted in his own club. The 'Red
Army' rationale for this rather un-Communist
behavior is that TSKA's facilities are expensive
and much in demand: a third-rate athlete may be
denying the use of these facilities to a better,
even a potentially world-beating sportsman.

But the army also developed a mass sports
organisation known as DOSAAF, the so-called
Voluntary Society for Aid to the Army Air Force

*Moscow University
gymnasium.*

and Navy. This is a vital civil defence organisation, giving rifle training to tens of millions of Russian youngsters, and generally prepares them for a future war. But it is as a sports organisation that it is most effective: 70 per cent of its subscriptions are channeled into sport and it has a wide range of standards which, unlike those of TSKA accommodate the abilities of most youngsters.

DOSAAF's aims were clearly spelled out in a Russian textbook recently: 'We aim to propagandise among the public especially young people, military knowledge and the heroic tradition of the Soviet people, to improve the quality of young people for service in the Armed Forces and to promote 'military-technical sports'.

What are 'military-technical' sports? Under the GTO scheme ('ready for labor and defence of the USSR') which acts as the measuring stick of mass sport performance – and which has been widely imitated in the rest of Eastern

Europe and Cuba – the 'military-technic[al] sports include the conventional Olympic ones[:] sprinting, long- and medium-distance runnin[g] swimming, high and long jumping and gymna[s-] tics. But there is also provision for less conve[n-] tional and more directly military sports – ski-i[ng] small-bore rifle shooting and hand-gren[ade] throwing. A 19 year-old woman would, [for] example, have to throw a 500 gramme gren[ade] (actually a similarly shaped chunk of wood) [x] metres before she could qualify for a gold me[dal] under the scheme.

DOSAAF, despite its 'voluntary' tag, is j[ust] about as compulsory as it is possible to be. [On] starting work at a factory or after changi[ng] schools, the newcomer is automatically reg[is-] tered on the DOSAAF lists and the subscripti[on] is docked from his salary. For the Commun[ist] sports juggernaut this has the advantage n[ot] only of teaching military skills – wearing a g[as] mask for one hour is one of the compulsory te[sts]

The complex of sport facilities at Russia's Central Army Sport Club.

out of providing a huge reserve of sporting
ent. A reserve moreover which can be legiti-
itely financed out of the coffers of the defence
dget and from the millions of 'voluntary' sub-
:riptions.

Yet there has been criticism of DOSAAF in
e Soviet press suggesting that the sports
structors do not take enough trouble with
erage children and that therefore the 'reserve'
not properly exploited.

There may be something in this. The majority
coaches and trainers clearly regard Dynamo
d TSKA as the peak of achievement and feel
at anything else is second-rate. But the two-
red system makes sense in many ways. It
stinguishes a more or less professional group

of sportsmen (in TSKA and Dynamo) from the
main body of the populace and can thus afford to
give them special treatment. These elite
sportsmen can then in turn act as an inspiration
for the masses, showing them that it is indeed
possible to become a 'New Socialist Man', the
ultimate goal of the Communist system. This too
is the approach in Communist economics in
general: factory workers who work especially
hard are given special privileges and are widely
publicised as a type of 'celebrity'.

Surprisingly, there seems to be little bitterness among sportsmen themselves about the
two-class system of sporting achievement. And
it really does appear to raise individual sporting
achievement: it allows Communist countries to

*The Sports Palace of the
Central Lenin Stadium.*

create sports stars in a system where everybody is supposed to be of equal importance to the state.

The military and the KGB perpetuate the two-tier approach by blurring the distinction between amateurs and professionals. Again Kiev Dynamo is the ideal illustration. It has been consistently portrayed as an amateur side – but it is professional by any normal measure. In and out of season, the players have their rent and keep paid and they receive generous salaries from their official employers, who are in turn recompensed by Dynamo (and thus indirectly by the KGB).

The West uses the military to allow sportsmen to keep their amateur status with the minimum of disruption to training schedules. This device is used mainly by the smaller and medium-ranking sporting countries, like Britain and Italy, to cover the costs of certain expensive sports and sometimes military-related sports.

The overwhelming majority of Western biathl (shooting and ski-ing) teams are soldiers, wh naval officers have traditionally been given ti off to practice for yachting events. A substan proportion of European riding teams is al accounted for by army officers. The US with complex system of university sports sholarshi has less need of the military device to clo covert professionalism.

The Soviet and East European background slightly different, but the justification for milita and KGB involvement is the same – how else you finance an increasingly expensive spo juggernaut so as to defend national prestige international events?

Initially, after the Revolution in Russia, milita or para-military organisation of sport ma sense: communications were bad and the arr seemed to be the only institution which cou bind the country together. Sports facilities we extremely scarce and so again military metho were a way of making efficient use of what w available.

The question of scarce resources is no long such a crucial one. But if the Communist cou tries are to retain their sporting prestige the have to be seen to be spending relatively litt money on sports. The USSR budget allocate only about 810 million roubles (the rouble roughly equivalent to the dollar) to health an physical culture (i.e. sport) and this grew rel tively slowly to about one billion roubles in 197 This was a decrease in real terms for the spor part of the allocation.

Some Western experts have pointed out th the relative share in the state budget in 1970 wa exactly the same (0.03 per cent) as it was in 192 when there were much more pressin priorities. Factory sporting funds push up th figure as does a curious institution known as th 'social insurance' fund. Under this scheme a organisations which hire labor contribute to th state social insurance. fund. Some of this is the allocated as sickness benefit while the rest goe on the financing of special sports school According to a recent Russian book on architec ture and sport, almost 60 per cent of the spor amenities under construction in the USSR wer being financed out of this insurance kitty.

None the less the brunt of sports sponsorshi falls on the KGB and the army. There is believe to be some resentment about this among the to brass of the military and the security service bu they still regularly increase the sporting alloca tions whose contributions effectively double th amount given directly by the state.

There are many ways in which the supporter of sport in the military command can justify thi

Top:
A new 'palace' for young budding gymnasts near western Siberia.

Below:
The rowing canal in Moscow.

h expenditure. In the first place, they argue, army has become far more efficient through sports scheme sponsorship by DOSAAF and East European equivalents. The average riod of national service in the Communist rld is about two years but if young men (and men) are taught how to throw hand gredes, how to shoot and how to fit gasmasks fore they even enter the army, then the fence effort is clearly going to be that much re efficient.

Sport moreover breeds the 'right' attitude to litary service: it forms the potential soldier's itude towards working in a team. 'Taking ders', said the Russian sports magazine seku Kultura recently, 'is that much easier for good sportsman.'

Taking orders is also an important attribute a disciplined workforce and there is evince that the military and sports machines rk closely with industrial enterprises. The 'O scheme carried out through the factory orkplace can, the Communists believe, cut wn absenteeism through illness. It can also ake workers more physically and mentally rt and thus raise productivity.

But above all factory-run sport is aimed at ckaging the increasing free time of workers d channeling it into a useful direction. 'More ortsmen – less dissidents' is the cry. If a facry scores higher than average marks in its orts tests then it usually earns a Communist rty recommendation and steals a march on her plants in the region. And this, in turn, rthers the careers of the factory management the successful plant.

One could argue of course that there is thing sinister or pre-planned about military d KGB involvement – that their participation mply reflects the dominant role of these institus in Communist society as a whole. The KGB, r example, has an estimated 90,000 staff offics and employs a further 400,000 personnel as erks, border guards and anti-terrorist troops. he number of additional spies and informants robably doubles this but the exact figure is mpossible to calculate. In addition there are bout four million uniformed Soviet soldiers. All this adds up to a formidable political force d it is natural, argue the Soviets, that these ind of numbers should be reflected in volvement in extra-curricular activities like ort. For many Russians – even non-official nes – it seems quite natural that the army hould be so active in sports. 'Soldiers are uman like us – why shouldn't they organise thletics matches,' commented one Russian migré to the authors.

Lavrenti Beria, ice-cool KGB leader — he fell victim to a purge shortly after Stalin's death in 1953.

Middle:
Russia's Olympic contingent in Rome.

Below:
The East Germany Dynamo club, a direct descendant of its Moscow namesake which is administered and funded largely by the KGB.

Training at Kiev Dynamo, one of the USSR's leading soccer clubs.

It is difficult not to see the justice of this view, though the sight of 12-year-olds throwing dummy hand grenades at sports tournaments is disturbing. What are they preparing for? War, claim some Western analysts who point out that the Russians have been traditionally afraid of encirclement by the 'capitalist West' and China and have always wanted to keep their population ready for another invasion like Hitler's in 1941.

It is less easy to explain away the KGB role and its strong presence at international tournaments is unsettling to say the least. At particularly sensitive international matches, KGB men are believed to make up about one-third of the total Soviet delegation. Similar proportions are turned out by the East Germans and the Bulgarians. Mostly they are disguised as supplementary officials or assistant coaches, as accompanying sports journalists or as chaperones for the girl teams. But some of the actual sportsmen and sportswomen – especially those from the Dynamo contingent – are also believed to be KGB informants.

Before they go abroad, Communist spo[rts]men and women are given strict instructio[ns] they must minimise all social contacts with fo[r]igners and they must report to their respect[ive] quarters at regular intervals, all sight-seeing [is] to be done in threes. One of the three is alm[ost] invariably a KGB informant, if not a full-ti[me] employee of the agency.

The whole emphasis of the KGB presence [at] tournments – especially the Olympics – is [to] prevent defections. The Communist countr[ies] have been particularly hit by defections fr[om] ballet companies abroad and sportsmen a[re] regarded as being open to the same temp[ta]tions.

The main lure for Communist sportsmen [to] defect is the prospect of excellent facilities a[nd] comparatively large salaries gleaned fr[om] advertising and other financial perks. Althou[gh] the Communist world has a comprehensive s[ys]tem of privilege for sportmen, it cannot comp[are] with the West in terms of financial rewards.

There are other enticements too. The you[ng] Russian diver Sergei who defected at t[he]

ntreal Olympics did so for the love of a adian girl. He went to ground for some days the Russians eventually insisted on talking to and persuaded him to return. Moscow used the West of deliberately setting up a duction' but although the Western intellig- services have certainly tried this in the it seems unlikely that they would have gone o much bother for the sake of a 17-year old r. The Russians, by all accounts used threats inst the diver's family in the USSR to per- de him to return: it is the relatives who can er most when sportsmen defect, as the ecting chess-player Viktor Korchnoi has covered. At the 1979 Wimbledon tennis tour- nent, Czech defector Martina Navratilova's her was allowed out of Czechoslovakia for first time to see her daughter play. It was an sual concession – but even so, Martina's

father had to stay at home so that his wife would return.

The Moscow Olympics presents a slightly different security problem for the KGB. It will be more difficult for the police to prevent meetings between foreigners and ordinary Russians but sportsmen will be kept on a tight rein and most foreigners will be confined to closely organised group schedules. There will not be much chance either of Communist defections: it would be almost impossible for an athlete to leave the country illegally, even tucked away in the boot of a foreign team's bus. The main thrust of KGB operations is Moscow will be to prevent illegal currency changing and black market dealing by the Russians and to prevent 'anti-Soviet' literature being distributed by foreign teams and other visitors.

Above:
Martina Navratilova
shares her 1979
Wimbledon triumph
with mother Jana.

Left:
Vladimir Makeev.

Right:
Verna of
Czechoslovakia,
developed as a
carbon copy of Olga
Korbut in the wake of
the latter's 1972
Olympic success.

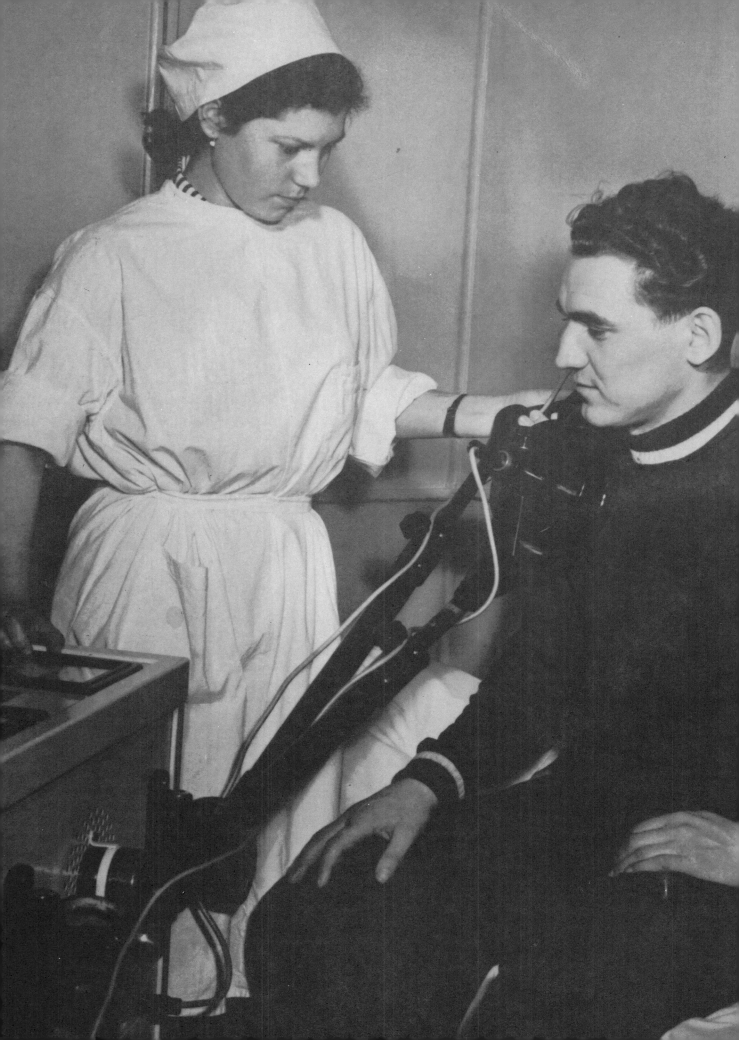

6 The Mechanics of Success

The System and the people
The System:

Communist governments are proud of the way they organise sport. There are sparkling new stadia, gyms, swimming pools, pitches and courts. Thousands of highly trained and sympathetic coaches help the masses reach physical – and mental – perfection through sport. Top class athletes compete in international events because they love the motherland and because they believe that sport helps destroy the artificial barriers of politics. And everyone, from the humblest weekend jogger to the Olympic gold medallist, realises that none of it would have been possible without Marx, Engels, Lenin and the Party.

That is roughly the picture of sport under Communism painted by the official sources. The reality of course is a little different. The figures issued for ordinaty people – the factory and office workers, the farmhands and peasants – taking any active interest in sport are grossly exaggerated, much as official figures for annual production or homes built are deliberately inflated. The official description of the quality of sports facilities available to the masses also owes more to the imagination of the propagandists than to facts. For the average Soviet or East German, someone who occasionally feels like a game of tennis or a workout in the gym, there are as many problems as for, say, a New Yorker or Londoner who suddenly decides it might be pleasant to play a game of squash. The sports facilities, and this is as true of rural areas as the major cities, are usually occupied by serious club athletes. In the West one needs money to buy time in gyms or on courts. In the East one really needs to be a member of a club. In fact,

this is probably not resented by the mass of people. As per capita income has risen in countries like the Soviet Union 'recreational' activities like fishing or camping have become more popular than mainstream sports. The majority now seem happy to hang up their running shoes and football boots after they leave school and, as in the West, are coming to depend on the television in their lounges to provide the ration of vicarious exercise.

The view of top class athletes is just as distorted and gives no hint of the philosophy that drives the Communist states to seek success in international sport or the ruthless methods used to achieve that success.

The Communist sports machine is most highly developed and least principled in Eastern Europe rather than in Cuba or China. To Western sports fans the sheer number of clubs, societies and institutes might suggest a comforting similarity to sport in their own countries – generally run without the interference of government. It is an illusion: sport like everything in Eastern Europe is controled by the Party and the state.

In the Soviet Union, the model for the rest of the Eastern Bloc, sport is organised by the All Union Committee on Physical Culture. This is based in Moscow and is attached to the Council of Ministers of the USSR; proof of the government's determination to keep a close watch on sport. The Committee occasionally issued edicts urging greater effort and more commitment; edicts which are directed at the fifteen committees controling sport in the republics. It was only set up in 1968 and replaced the All Union Council of Trade Unions as the supreme sports authority of the Soviet Union. Until that reorganisation most workers had belonged to their trade union sports society – like the car

World Record Holders

Record at November 1979	Record at November 1979	Record at November 1979	Record at November
Koch	Krause	Khristov	Riehm
East Germany	*East Germany*	*Bulgaria*	*East Germany*
21·71 secs.	55·41 secs.	645·0 Kg.	80·32 metres

1976	**1976**	***1976**	**1976**
Eckert	Ender	Zaitsev	Sedyh
East Germany	*East Germany*	*U.S.S.R.*	*U.S.S.R.*
22·37 secs.	55·65 secs.	590.5 Kg.	77·52 metres
1972	**1972**	**1972**	**1972**
Stecher	Neilsen	Talts	Bondartschuck
East Germany	*U.S.A.*	*U.S.S.R.*	*U.S.S.R.*
22·4 secs.	58·59 secs.	580·0 Kg.	75·50 metres
1968	**1968**	**1968**	**1968**
Szewinska	Henne	Shabotinsky	Oerter
Poland	*U.S.A.*	*U.S.S.R.*	*U.S.A.*
22·5 secs.	1 min.	572·5 Kg.	64·78 metres
1964	**1964**	**1964**	**1964**
McGuire	Fraser	Shabotinsky	Oerter
U.S.A.	*Australia*	*U.S.S.R.*	*U.S.A.*
23·0 secs.	59·5 secs.	572·5 Kg.	61·0 metres
1960	**1960**	**1960**	**1960**
Rudolph	Fraser	Vlassov	Oerter
U.S.A.	*Australia*	*U.S.S.R.*	*U.S.A.*
24·0 secs.	1 min. 1·2 secs.	537·5 Kg.	59·18 metres
1956	**1956**	**1956**	**1956**
Cuthbert	Fraser	Anderson	Oerter
Australia	*Australia*	*U.S.A.*	*U.S.A.*
23·4 secs.	1 min. 2 secs.	500·0 Kg.	56·36 metres
1952	**1952**	**1952**	**1952**
Jackson	Szöke	Davis	Iness
Australia	*Hungary*	*U.S.A.*	*U.S.A.*
23·7 secs.	1 min. 6·8 secs.	460·0 Kg.	53·03 metres
1948	**1948**	**1948**	**1948**
Blankers-Koen	Andersen	Davis	Consolini
Holland	*Denmark*	*U.S.A.*	*Italy*
24·4 secs.	1 min. 6·3 secs.	452·5 Kg.	52·78 metres

Olympic Winners (between each column)

Running
Womens 200 Metres

Swimming
Womens 100 Metres Freestyle

Weightlifting
Heavyweight

Mens Hammer

(2 hands press, 2 hands snatch, 2 hands jerk)

*From 1976 2 hands press was dropped from
the weightlifting contest, and an estimation
of the rate of progress has been made.

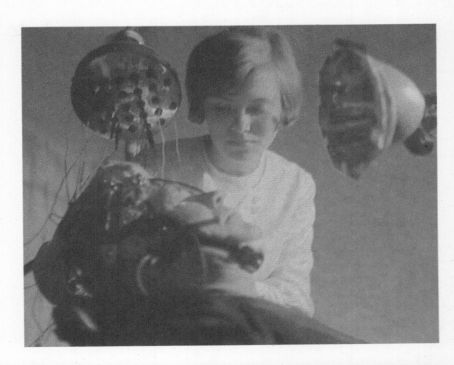

low:
antorena of Cuba
nning 800 m final
Montreal.

workers' Torpedo union or the canal workers' Vodnik union. Now most belong to their republican union, called Trud in the Russian Republic and Avangrad in the Ukraine. A few trade union societies remained intact – notably the KGB financed Dynamo club and Central Red Army Club.

These bodies are one cog of the machine. Another is the para-military civil defence body DOSAAF (Voluntary Society for Aid to the Army, Air Force and the Navy). Its main role is in running a set of sports awards called the GTO badges (Ready for Defence and Labor). DOSAAF has 65 million members aged between 15 to 26 – apparently indicating a wholehearted love of sport by Soviet youth. But membership happens to be as near compulsory as makes no difference and only a small proportion of the 65 million take any real interest in the society's activities, which include 'sports' like parachute jumping and military exercises.

Sports clubs at factories and farm collectives are also vital to the smooth functioning of the machine, providing a home base for thousands of athletes. And the wealthy Dynamo and army clubs help by training athletes in high cost sports like rowing or ice hockey. The whole complex has only one object – to produce and support top class athletes.

One of the main strengths of the system lies i the schools: in ensuring that gifted children ar spotted early by coaches. Some youngsters ma be earmarked for special treatment before the have even enroled in primary school – girl gym nasts, for example, are often sent from nurser school to a sports school. In East Berlin elit clubs like TSC or SC Dinamo frequently adver tise for 'new little stars' from four years old on One East German athlete who defected said: 'A the SC club it was quite usual to see four-year old children on the ice. They take the skater very early . . .'

In the ordinary schools children follow th official 'physical culture syllabus' drawn up b central government. According to the Soviet this develops 'moral and physical qualities' and inculcates 'patriotism, purposefulness, interna tionalism, team work and self assurance'. In th Soviet Union, as in the rest of the Eastern Bloc the sports timetable is based on awards organ ised by the Civil Defence Organisation. The authorities fix 'achievement quotas' for each school. Soviet schools are, for instance, told tha every normal child between the ages of 10 and 15 must win at least one GTO badge. Mos schools fulfil or exceed the targets set; in the same way that factories or farm collectives always proudly announce that they have beaten oduction targets whether it is true or not. ...metimes the authorities decide that the statis-...al charade is getting out of control and allow ...ne criticism of the blatantly inaccurate fig-...es. The last attacks were made in the early ...venties when a sports administrator said that ...ly a 'quarter of our children play sport regu-...ly' and the newspaper *Pravda* said that only ...per cent of children played any sport outside ...nool.

...Despite the widespread apathy and the rig-...ng of the minor sports awards Soviet and East ...ropean schools do give potential athletes a ...ance to display their talents. Any child that ...n genuinely climb the GTO ranking ladder – ...d coaches and teachers know as well as any-...e which awards are deserved – must have ...lity. The tests are tough and wide ranging. A ...year-old boy going for his GTO Stage 3 badge ...s to run sprint and middle distance races, ...np, throw and ski, cycle and swim. He must ...ve a 'thorough knowledge of physical culture ...d sport,' be able to carry out 'personal ...giene' and explain the importance of 'morn-...g exercises.' He must also be able to 'perform ...e initial military training programme.'

...Promising youngsters are recommended to ...e local sports schools for extra training. These 'children and young people's sports schools' vary considerably in character. In the larger, wealthier cities they may have their own elaborate training complexes; in the smaller towns and more remote rural areas they may have to make do with hired pools, gyms and running tracks.

The coaches sift out the potentially top class athletes by pushing classes through punishing training sessions. In one Moscow sports school 11-year-olds had to practice for two hours a night three times a week – usually after a hard day at ordinary school. In another sports school a 15-year-old trained for sixteen hours a week. When Olga Korbut began serious training at a local sports school she was immediately given star treatment. Two experienced women gymnasts, doctors and choreographers dedicated themselves to turning the latest child prodigy into an Olympic gold medallist. By the time she was 10 Korbut was spending more time training than studying or playing.

The pressure is intense on these youngsters. They know that they have to maintain their progress if they are to have any chance of being admitted to the elite full-time sports schools or sports boarding schools. And that progress is cruelly charted for them by the GTO awards and

Right:
The Central Army Club figure skating school for children in Moscow.

by the state's junior ranking table. Certainly they cannot complain that the system neglects them: in the Soviet Union over half the country's qualified coaches work in sports or special sports schools.

One only needs to look at the number of Communist athletes who began their careers in these schools to realise that the investment has not been wasted.

East European parents know that there other ways – apart from athletic ability – for th children to impress the coaches. Every Co munist party in Eastern Europe has a childre wing – like the Soviet Union's Young Pioneer that organises summer camps and work p jects. Parents know that it is important that th children show exemplary enthusiasm for the often tiresome activities. It is even more imp

Russia's Valery Shary acknowledges his debt to good fortune after winning a gold at Montreal.

Below: Former Olympic champion Grant Shaginian training children at a sports school in Yerevan.

96

tant that they apply to the youth wing of the party when they are old enough. In the Soviet Union teenagers know that becoming a member of the Young Communist League gives them social status, and assures the authorities that they are committed Communists. It also gives them a good chance of one day being accepted by the Party itself – still considered a rare privilege behind the Iron Curtain. 'I don't know anyone

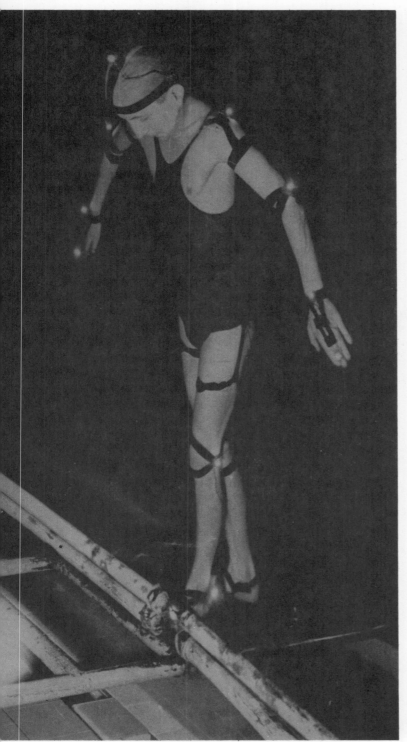

...eshkov swimming ... lighted bulbs on ...ry joint to facilitate ...ntific study of the ...mmer in action.

who joins the Komsomol (Young Communist League) out of conviction,' one Russian teenage girl told an American correspondent. Another student complained that he had been accused of being a counter revolutionary because he was not a Komsomol member.

Only a fraction of the hopefuls training at the sports schools – over a million in the Soviet Union alone – manage to climb to the next rung of the ladder.

In the Soviet Union some of the lucky ones are sent to the full-time sports schools, where perhaps thirty hours a week is spent training and only fifteen hours on academic work. The child wonders are sent to sports boarding schools – the most prestigious of all sports schools. The East Germans set up the first of these but the Soviet Union soon followed, building the first in Tashkent in 1962. There are now 20 of them with another 24 planned. The increasing elitism of sport in East European schools – concentrating on excellence by a few rather than competence for all – has been attacked by some brave, outspoken teachers. One said that she had tried to teach her pupils to 'love beauty, value friendship and appreciate hard work.' The school inspectors, she said, were only interested in the number of children who had won sports awards. 'We gallop after these rankings without stopping to think what we are doing. Scarcely is a child out of the cradle than we fix his fate as a Master of Sport. Yet how many children are thrown overboard in our race for results.' But criticism like this, which can jeopardise a teacher's entire career, is rare and ineffectual.

The sports boarding schools usually select their pupils at the local and national spartakiads – games that are closely modeled on the Olympics. Sometimes, however, a school may advertise in the sports press asking for children to come forward for tests – a safety measure in the unlikely event that a potential champion has escaped the net.

Most recruits – generally aged between 7 and 13 – then have to pass a searching ten-day examination. Doctors and psychiatrists, teachers and coaches probe for fatal flaws, mental as well as physical, that would lead to inevitable failure. There are no figures showing how many, are rejected at this stage.

If they pass the examination parents are asked to sign release papers that allow the state to take charge of the child. Of course this is a formality. A few cunning parents have been known to extract a car or new flat from the authorities in return for letting their children join a sports school. That requires delicate and dangerous negotiation and a fine understanding of Communist bureaucracy so most simply sign the release forms, consoling themselves with the thought that their child has a chance of becoming a privileged member of society.

So far the elite sports schools have concentrated on the Olympic sports because, argue the politicians, it is through the Olympics that athletes most clearly prove their world supremacy. With the growing importance of sports like tennis the syllabus may be widened. For the moment schools tend to specialise in three or four sports: the Tallinn special sports school in the Soviet Union teaches football, athletics, swimming and gymnastics whilst the Tashkent school admits only young footballers, swimmers, athletes and gymnasts. Big city schools tend to be well equipped with indoor and outdoor pools, gyms, tracks and medical facilities. In one Moscow school there are seven Merited Coaches of Sport of the USSR and twelve Masters of Sport on the coaching staff. It is a different story in the provinces. At the Rostov or Don school it was reported in the early seventies that there was only one shot for every ten putters and no stop watches for the runners.

Little is left to chance. Doctors devise special diets for each pupil, knowing that they can order as much fresh meat or fruit as they want even if there are food shortages in the area. There are regular medical checks and free trips to exclusive holiday resorts. Everything is paid for by the state but the sacrifices asked of the pupils, many of whom are eight or nine years old, are considerable.

Training increases over the years until, by the time they are 16 or 17, they are in all but name full-time professional athletes. The strain shows in the high failure rate – put as high as 60 per cent by some experts but probably nearer 25 to 30 per cent. This, however, will not deter the authorities who remain convinced that elite training of children is a proven method of achieving world dominance in sport.

Once they are 18 years old, athletes at the special or sports boarding schools have to move

A rather primitive w massage system, vintage 1949

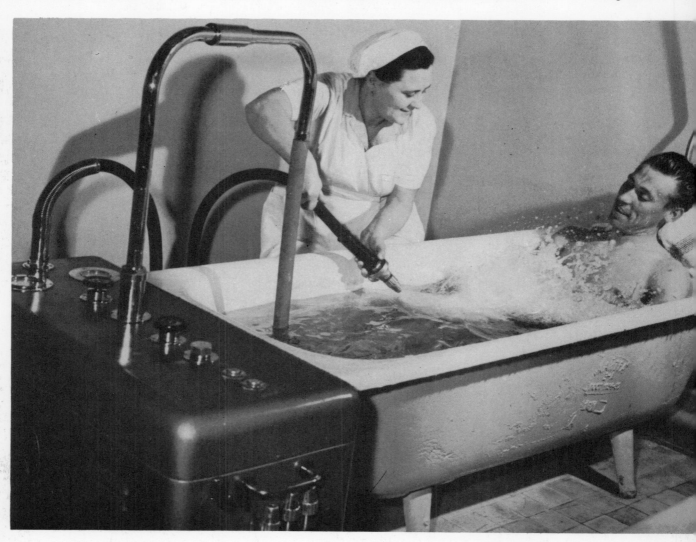

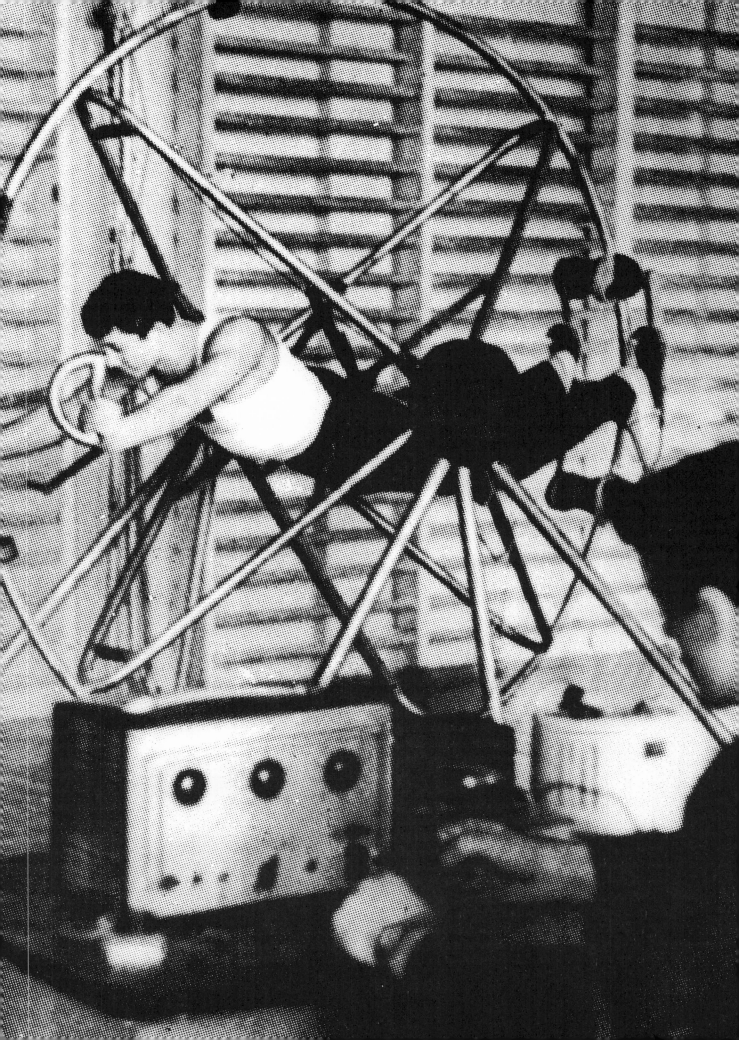

on. At that age most of their contemporaries have to worry about finding a job, avoiding the draft or being accepted by a university or college of further education. For the elite athletes life is simpler – providing that they have trained and competed well and have done as they were told. Some are assigned to factories or farm collectives; nominal jobs which give them a reasonable salary and allow them to continue full-time training and competition. Most go on to institutes of physical culture and sport or colleges specialising in sports degrees.

In the Soviet Union the most talented athletes are sent to one of the country's 20 institutes of physical culture and sport. If they are lucky then they are allowed to read for the coveted degree of 'sports instructor'. This guarantees them a top class coaching job when they retire. If they are less fortunate they read for the degree of 'teacher of physical culture and sport' – which only allows them to coach in colleges, schools, sports societies and farm and factory collectives.

At the Soviet Union's leading institutes – The State Order of Lenin Institute in Moscow and the Lesgaft Institute in Leningrad – students only read for the higher of the two degrees. They are the *crème de la crème*, the elite of the elite. Despite the gap in status in the two degrees the syllabuses are almost identical: Communist philosophy, psychology, hygiene, biochemistry as well as sports training techniques. For many graduates of the special sports schools the future is not so bright. They are sent to physical education faculties or secondary physical culture colleges before being assigned to low level teaching posts.

East German teenagers are also dispersed when they leave the special sports schools. A few are sent to the German Academy of Physical Culture at Leipzig University – one of the world's leading research and training centres and described by one British academic as 'one of the most remarkable institutions in the whole of the German Democractic Republic. . . unique in its treatment of physical culture and there is probably no college in the whole world that can stand comparison with it.' It was founded in 1950 with just 96 students and 14 coaches. Now it has over 2000 full time students who stay in residence for four years. There are ten sports halls, a giant swimming pool, running tracks, football and hockey pitches, and lecture halls. The East Germans encourage foreign, and especially Third World athletes, to study there on scholarships – rightly believing that helping a country develop in sport is as good a means as any of making new allies.

Left:
Russia's Nina Ponomareva breakin the Olympic women's discus record at Rome, 1960.

Below:
Soviet cycle racer Viktor Kapitonov (le outsprinting an Italia rival at the finish of th individual road race Rome, 1960.

A day at the Youth Sports School for Fencing in Kiev.

is fitting that the other supremely elitist
rts centre in East Germany stands within
ing distance of the academy. Lying on the
er bank of the River Elster the Sports Club
senschaft has between 2400 to 2500 gradu-
s – men and women who form the heart of the
ntry's athletic strength.

hey are at the apex of the sports pyramid.
letes are on a cash bonus scheme when they
pete in major international events: the
gest bonus is paid when they beat Ameri-
s, the smallest when they beat a fellow
nmunist. An Olympic gold is worth around
,000 and possibly a new car, flat or lucrative

Breaking records can also swell athletes'
lets. The swimmer Roland Matthes, 100 and
metres back-stroke champion at Munich,
rumoured to always hold himself back
en he broke a record, knowing that he would
able to improve on the performance and so
n another hefty bonus. Shot puttter Margitta
mmel was seen driving a smart new sports

car – as prestigious in East Germany as owning
a Rolls-Royce is in England – after her gold
medal success in Mexico. the number plate was
SC 1961: SC for her club and 1961 to commemo-
rate her winning throw of 19.61 metres. Athletes
like Matthes and Gummel are, barring some
catastrophic mistake, guaranteed a place within
the elite for the rest of their lives. It may be in
coaching or administration but one thing is certain, they will not be uncomfortable or over-
worked.

The Cubans too are becoming more and
more concerned with early selection and elite
training. In 1969 Fidel Castro handed over an
entire island – the Island of Pines to the south of
the mainland – for development as a centre for
specialist secondary schools. There are now 28
semi-residential and residential schools and
over 10,000 pupils there studying everything
from shot putting, high jumping and sprinting to
physics, mathematics and economics.

The most brilliant pupils though are sent to

the Lenin School on the outskirts of the capital Havana. Few Westerners have been allowed to visit the school, perhaps because it is the epitome of the elitism that party doctrine insists disappeared along with capitalism in the revolution of 1959. The government pours resources into the Lenin School to ensure that the 4500 pupils there do not suffer any of the shortages still endemic in Cuba. There are, for example, only a handful of all weather running tracks in the country but the school has international class indoor and outdoor arenas, as well as swimming pools, gyms, basketball, volleyball and baseball courts.

But it is not just in its treatment of child and teenage talent that Cuba mirrors Eastern Europe. There is an all-powerful central authority with close links with government, just as there is in the Soviet Union. This body – the Instituto de Deportes Educacion Fisica y Recreacion, commonly know as INDER – is based in Havana and is part of an extraordinary sports complex that includes the National Training Centre, the Institute of Sports Medicine, the Physical Education Institute and many of the factories of Cuba's nationalised sports equipment industry.

The East European pattern is also followed in the schools: compulsory sport for all and sports awards to help coaches spot promising athletes. There are the Junior Olympics – modeled on the Spartakiads. But significantly there is little evidence of the corruption and cynicism that is so pervasive in the East. Many teachers and coaches appear to be working for enjoyment and love of sport rather than material rewards. And the young stars on the Island of Pines or at the Lenin School, if not established internationals like the boxer Teofilo Stevenson, lead lives that are less cosseted and secret than their counterparts in the East. They are often allowed to go home at weekends and academic standards, certainly compared to schools in East Germany or the Soviet Union, are more rigorously enforced.

Of course the official Cuban policy is to use sport to bring equality. But the expanding sports machine $60 million worth of government aid in 1975 – is designed to produce Olympic champions rather than fit farmers or factory workers.

What of China – third largest country in the world? during the late fifties and sixties there was limited interest in Chinese sport, understandably since she was only sporadically and half-heartedly involved in international competition.

In the early seventies the Irishman Lord Killanin became President of the International Oly-

mpic Committee and made it his ambition to persuade China back into the Olympic fold. By then China through basketball and table tennis, the so-called 'ping pong diplomacy', had tentatively resumed contact with the rest of the world. In 1978 China came second overall – behind Japan – in the Asian Games in Bangkok. In 1979 she was asked to take her place in the Olympic movement renounced in 1958 in protest over Taiwan's membership. Later that year a Chinese official told the international news agencies that his country would like to host the 1988 Olympics. Now Western and indeed East European experts began to debate whether China had the necessary organisation to exploit the untapped resources of her huge population.

Right:
Tough training for
Russian long-distan
runner Piotr Bolotri
1960.

There are clearly problems comparing China with any of the East European states. Her culture is a baffling mix: oriental and conservative yet also radical and sometimes fanatic. In its administration of sport, and this is misleading, China appparently resembles the Soviet Union, with whom she once had strong ties. Strong government controled bodies oversee local organisations, schools and party groups. Schoolchildren aim for awards under the National Physical Training Programme – awards modeled on the Soviet GTO badges and which include the usual para-military exercises like genade throwing. There are sports schools too, 1500 in all, designed to provide a steady stream of top class athletes. And there are the familiar Communist pronouncements on the purpose of sport: to build a strong healthy nation ready to defend their country against foreign invaders.

But the differences are fundamental. The mass exercise programme of Chairman Mao Tse Tung has no parallel in Eastern Europe. Mao decided that modern sport, even if it was only early morning push-ups; would help lift China into the 20th century. He showed the way with his remarkable swims across rivers like the Yangtze, swims which he persisted with into an obese old age. The feats have become legendary and Western tourists always marvel at the thousands of boys and girls, mothers and pensioners who regularly plunge in rivers on long distance swims. Westerners are astonished too at the number performing early morning exercises. 'Peking in the early morning is alive with joggers and exercisers and people playing badminton over imaginary nets. There are bicy-

A Russian shot-putter wired to monitor reflexes and muscle-stress.

cles everywhere,' reported one Western analyst when he was discussing the general Chinese commitment to physical fitness.

Chinese children are encouraged to enjoy themselves rather than to compete and succeed. 'Commandism and formalism' say the authorities stiffly, are evils confined to the regimes of Eastern Europe. This does not of course mean that Chinese schoolchildren develop in quite the same way as American or British youngsters. Sport, insist the doctrinaires, develops a 'worker's consciousness and culture' – which is hardly the idea of baseball in American high schools or cricket in English public schools.

Children accepted by one of the country's 1500 spare-time sports schools are spared the intense pressures endured by promising Soviet or East German children. 'In the Soviet Union the relationship between a coach and an athlete like Olga Korbut is very much one of command and response. In China the relationship seems much more relaxed,' wrote one journalist.

This should not imply that the Chinese are taking their famous motto– Friendship First, Competition Second – too seriously. 'Yes we still think that but we already have friendship. .' quipped one Chinese coach to an American trainer. It is true that more children are being selected early, especially in gymnastics and table tennis, but the methods used to train them do not, for the time being at least compare with those employed in other Communist states.

If China is to fully recover from the isolationism of the past then much will depend on the country's eight institutes of physical culture. During the reign of the Gang of Four, when most sports and all forms of competition were branded as bourgeois and decadent – the institutes were left to fall derelict. Coaches and athletes were sent to the provinces to be 're-educated' in the fields and their places taken by party zealots who knew nothing about sport.

In the last year or so the institutes have begun to build up again. At the Peking institute, lavishly equipped with swimming pools, running tracks,

A gymnastics lesson a Children's Sports School in Leningrad.

ns, courts and shooting ranges, students
ve started to return. But unlike their collea-
es in Eastern Europe students cannot expect
terial rewards that would set them apart from
mass of workers. This is true too after they
alify as coaches. They are paid average
ges – which is to say not very much – and do
receive the free cars, flats or Western
thes that are taken for granted by the East
ropean elite.

e People

Sometimes the elite athletes of Eastern
rope want something more than comfortable,
vileged lives in a closed society. And in those
ses they usually have only one option – to
fect to the West.

For the Communist authorities and security
vices defections by leading athletes are dis-
erous and humiliating and the efforts to stop
m are constantly reviewed. After each
portant defection the security forces try to
prove their screening methods, hoping to
sure that potential defectors are spotted
fore it is too late. They step up surveillance on
ups travelling abroad and some sources now
ckon that on average one third of every
mmunist sports party in the West now consist
security agents. But the steady trickle of
letes fleeing to the West continues and will
ntinue to do so for as long as life under capital-
is for many a more attractive proposition
n life under Communism.

The privileged members of Communist
cieties find defecting relatively easy. These
ters, artists, government officials, scientists,
let dancers, musicians and athletes know the
est. Many have made friends there who prom-
to help them adjust to their new homeland.
st important of all they have the oppor-
ities. They do not have to risk being cut down
machine gun fire whilst trying to find a way
er the walls, pits and minefields of the Berlin
all. They do not have to risk being discovered
a border guard hiding in the false bottom of a
r. They can simply walk to freedom during a
it to London, Paris of New York.

The authorities do their best to shrug off the
ses. In the case of, say, a writer who has fled
the West the propaganda machine works
ickly and effectively. Little can be done in the
est, apart perhaps from suggesting that the
iter was a sexual deviant or a black mar-
teer. More can be done at home. The masses
told that the writer was reactionary and
urgeois; a liability whom the state is better off

without. But then the masses rarely identify with
writers or ballet dancers and they do not particularly miss them.

It is more inconvenient when the defector is a
well-known and popular athlete. The authorities
can always try to ignore the whole affair. If they
do that the American run radio stations in West
Germany broadcasting to the Warsaw Pact will
make sure that the oversight is corrected. The
propagandists can accuse the athlete of leaving
to escape pending criminal charges: sometimes
for a sexual crime, perhaps for espionage, but
always for something repulsive. All this, however, is doublethink in the best traditions of
George Orwell's 1984. It is impossible for the
authorities to successfully blacken the name of
an athlete who was, only a few days before,
hailed as the paragon of Socialist virtues, a
champion of the brave new Communist world.

Chairman Mao taking to water.

Viktor Bushvev jerking a new world and Olympic record 150 kilos for Russia, in the lightweight division at Rome, 1960.

Occasionally the ice cold Communist facade cracks. This happened in 1976 during the Montreal Olympics when the 17 year old Soviet diver Sergei Nemtsanov disappeared from the athletes' village. The Soviets played straight in to the hands of the Western press: they demanded that the boy be returned, accused 'third parties' of abducting and brainwashing him. As the hours passed the Soviets became even more hysterical and threatened to withdraw from the games if Nemtsanov was not returned. This was an empty threat. The Soviets were not about to throw away the chance of 'winning' the Olympics – as far as they are concerned the world championship of sport – purely because one young diver had defected. When Nemtsanov was located the Soviet outburst appeared totally absurd and unreasoning. The boy had not been kidnapped. He had fallen in love with a Canadian girl

Most defections are more subdued affairs warranting only a paragraph or two in the world's press. The list is lengthy and the pattern a well-established one of athletes slipping quietly away from their teams and asking for political asylum.

In 1973, during the prestigious Milk Race in Britain, the Rumanian cyclists Josif Naghi, aged 19, and Zoltan Elekes, aged 20, left their comrades in Plymouth, Devon, hitchhiked to London and asked if they could stay in the West. One year later the Czech ice hockey captain Vaclav Nedomansky went one better – escaping to the West with his wife and children. It was reported that he had spent years planning the move, slowly convincing the authorities that he was dedicated enough Communist to be given a family visa. Once he was safely in Switzerland he announced that he was cutting his holiday short and that he and his family would be flying on to Canada. The experience taught the Communist security forces to be even more cautious about issuing family visas for travel abroad.

Most defectors are not as lucky as Nedomansky. They have to leave close relatives behind – knowing that they will be punished in their absence. Czech tennis star Martina Navratilova, who defected to the West when she was 18 years old, knows this only too well. Her mother Jana was not allowed to travel to the West to see her daughter play until 1979. That trip – to the Wimbledon championships in London – was widely reported throughout the world and seemed to indicate that the Czech authorities had at last softened. This feeling was reinforced when the Czechs said highlights of Martina's games would be shown on television. The story even appeared to have the proverbial happy ending when Martina won the women's singles title for the second year running. 'I hope now that they will eventually let my family leave Czechoslavakia and come to America to live with me,' she said after her victory. Her young stepsister, Jana, probably felt much the same. A talented tennis player herself, she was being denied practice time by the authorities who doubtless did not want another tennis star in the same, very troublesome family.

A few days after Martina's Wimbledon triumph another Czech tennis star, the teenager Hana Strachanova, defected. Strachanova, who was playing in the Swiss Open at Gstaad, asked for political asylum and vowed never to return home. Strachanova – rated as one of the most promising women players in the world after her performances earlier that year in the French and German championships – said simply that she could earn more money in the West. The reaction from the Czech security services, already waging a bitter war against the liberals who had been protesting over the abuse of human rights in their country, was predictable. They reviewed and tightened arrangements for allowing athletes out of Communist controled areas of Europe. And any hopes of an exit visa for the Navratilova family were, of course, dashed.

Pupils of the Yerevan school for young gymnasts in training.

Many defectors refuse to discuss their reasons for leaving the East, hoping no doubt that refusing to attack the system will help relatives still living behind the Iron Curtain. Some may even fear for their own safety; by no means an extravagent idea considering the fate of Bulgarian exile Georgi Markov, killed by the Bulgarian or Soviet security forces whilst he was working for the BBC World Services in London.

Consequently many defectors refuse to speak to the Western press. Some give curt, one line answers that are buried inside the newspaper pages. Others, like Strachanova, give cheap, glib reasons for defecting which seem to almost exonerate the Communist authorities. The 22 year old rower Walter Lambertus said that he had 'left for freedom' after his defection during the Montreal Olympics. In 1978 Rumanian boxer Mircea Simon said that he had never had any choice in his life.'I was told that I was going to be a boxer and I became a boxer.' Other defectors said that 'life under Communism does not allow one to live like a human being'; that there was a 'general air of oppression' and that they had 'left to find freedom'.

A few Communist athletes manage to find the best of both worlds: to live in the West without having to suffer the traumas of defection. Tennis player Ilie Nastase has never actually defected,

Both the coach and his 2-year old protegé take the game seriously.

despite his considerable wealth and exuberant lifestyle. He reached a compromise long ago with the Rumanian authorities who allow him to play and live abroad providing that he continues to play Davis Cup matches for them.

Nastase sensibly refuses to ever discuss politics. In his recent and highly acclaimed biography on Nastase, Richard Evans wrote: 'this is a story about a tennis player – and an apolitical one at that. Nastase is not unaware of what goes on in his own country and he has his own opinions about it. But he knows he has been placed in a highly privileged position and he genuinely feels he can better serve his family, friends and himself by maintaining his ties with Rumania . . . Under the present arrangement a great deal of self-serving pragmatism is being exercised by both sides . . No one is harmed by it and Nastase and the Rumanian authorities are by no means the only parties to reap the rewards . . . Anyone wishing to blow the whistle should remember that'.

In another passage Mr. Evans hints at the fascinating relationship of the showman tennis player and the Communist state when he describes Nastase's hesitation in accepting an invitation to play for Rumania in a Davis Cup match in Bucharest. 'On the face of it, that was not much to ask for what Nastase was getting in return, as he was allowed to keep all his world wide earnings; travel as and where he pleased, and even obtain permission to take both his parents to France for extended holidays.' Nastase's complaints – he would miss a lucrative American tournament – were muted and he returned to Bucharest. He still had, it must be remembered, many close relatives, living in Rumania.

His wife Dominique, however, refused to travel with him. '. .she was suffering from some quite illogical fear that the Rumanian authorities might somehow try to keep the child (their daughter Nathalie) in the country. The only logical answer to that was that governments can be stupid but not that stupid" says Mr. Evans. The reader is left to ponder and peer at photographs of the long haired Nastase in his uniform as a Rumanian army major.

Unfortunately for the Communist governments not all athletes are so co-operative. The stories of two in particular – the East Germans Dr. Alois Mader and Renate Neufeld – revealed the ruthless efficiency with which the Eastern European countries were pursuing sporting supremacy.

There has probably never been a more remarkable success story in the long history of sport than of the German Democratic Republic.

In 1949 the country lay in ruins, materially and spiritually. The cities had been devastated by war and the people were demoralised and bewildered by invasion and then partition. It is now the second most powerful Communist state in sport, lagging only marginally behind the Soviet Union. Despite having a population of just 17 million – compared to the 200 million plus of the Soviet Union and United States and the 50 million plus of the United Kingdom – it finished second in the Montreal medals table.

Its squad of 175 men and 117 women won 40 gold, 25 silver and 25 bronze medals. The women did especially well, taking more than half the team's 90 medals. And overall they won more medals than all the other women at the games put together. Yet at Tokyo Olympics in 1964 East Germany managed only 16 medals. At Mexico four years later they won 25 medals. The real jump came at Munich. in 1972 where they took 66 medals, including 20 golds. By 1976 they were more powerful than the United States and were able to dominate events that they had never before seriously contended. In swimming, for example, East German woman won 18 medals. Four years before they had gone home empty handed.

How can this incredible progress be explained? The propagandists point to the general dedication to sport in East Germany. The masses, they say, provide the base for success. This is clearly nonsense. In 1965, in percentage terms, fewer people played sport regularly than in West Germany – which won only 39 medals in Montreal. Nor is the structure of East German sport markedly different from that of other Soviet satellites: early selection, elite training and privilege. The difference lies in the people operating the system. They are better at selecting young athletes; more ruthless in training them; totally uncompromising when faced with failure. They are driven too by a desire to win that is matched only in the Soviet Union. There the enemy is America; in East Germany it is West Germany. The commitment is total with the government allocating the same proportion of its budget to elite sport as the British government does to education.

Dr. Alois Mader had been head of research at the Chemie Club in Halle for six years when he defected to the West with his wife and daughter in the mid seventies. It was a nightmare defection for the East Germans. It was bad enough that Dr. Mader was an experienced senior official who had first had knowledge of secret selection and training methods. It was made intolerable by the fact that his wife and daughter had escaped with him. Dr. Mader, the security

forces told furious government officials, could not be effectively silenced by threats to his family. Dr. Mader made the most of his opportunity and gave Western analysts a uniquely coherent picture of the East German sports machine.

He told one British newspaper that he had left because he could no longer tolerate the inhumanity of the system. In the West, he said, athletes were at least free to decide whether they succeeded or failed. 'The state does not buy you from your parents and force you to do things. If you want to drive yourself to the limit then you can. The state does not punish you for failure. it does not use you to boost its own sense of achievement. It does not force you to take drugs!'

Chemie was and is typical of elite East German sports clubs: hundreds of top class athletes in full time training, superb facilities, dozens of coaches and doctors and research staff.

One of Dr. Mader's tasks was to assess the potential of youngsters who had been spotted by club coaches. Perhaps his most remarkable patient was a young swimmer called Kornelia Ender – later to win four gold medals at Montreal. Ender, who had been in full time training since she was eight years old, was brought to Mader when she was 13. After analysing the blood samples he had taken from her ear lobes Dr. Mader told the delighted coaches that the girl was a potential Olympic champion. She was immediately tested in one of the treadmill-like machines used to judge a swimmers fitness. 'They have to swim against a variable current produced by a blade. She had to stay in the same place and from that we could judge her potential. She lasted longer than anyone. We calculated that she swum the equivalent to a 58 second 100 metres. The world record at that time was 58.5 seconds but we told her that would not be good enough at Montreal. By then we told her she would be swimming 56 seconds. You must understand that nothing is left to chance. The athletes have no choice in the matter,' explained Dr. Mader. Ender, of course did as she was ordered and won the Montreal 100 metres in 56 seconds.

Western experts were also intrigued to learn that computers were playing a major role in the selection and training of elite athletes. Personal judgement by trainers was, it seemed, being replaced by the objective infallibility of machines.

Ender, for example, had first been judged by computer when she was nine. 'She was tested for height, weight, lung capacity, things like that. The results were then compared with the computer's measurements of potential,' said Dr.

Mader. The Berlin computer also dictated the numbers admitted to special sports schools. In swimming it calculated that 1,100 eight, nine and ten year olds needed to be taken into training to produce between six and seven Olympic medallists. The process, however, would take seven years. 'There is no sentiment. It was worked out by the computer that you needed to take in so many at the bottom to produce one winner. 90 per cent of the children were dropped within five years'. Every year, added Dr. Mader, children are set targets by the computer. If they failed to reach them they were sent back to ordinary schools, and the chance of ever becoming a member of the sports elite had, except on rare occasions, disappeared.

The computer had other roles too. 'One of my colleagues was given the job of finding the next Olympic marathon champion. The computer was fed all the details and came up with the description of the man needed to win. 'The computer's conclusions were compared with the record of every athlete on the state's books and Waldemar Cierpinski emerged. Three years later Cierpinski won the Montreal marathon. The computer was even helpful in spotting East German weaknesses. After Munich it was asked how East Germany could be sure of dominating the rowing in 1976. The answer came back – five per cent more training. In Montreal East Germany won nine gold medals in rowing.

Children who survive to become first class athletes have little freedom. 'We knew everything about them. In effect we took them to pieces to find out how they worked'. In return for giving up the basic freedoms of deciding what they ate, when they slept and how hard they trained, athletes were, said Dr. Mader, given prizes, money and goods'. Ender had, he added, inevitably become rich after Montreal. 'She was introduced at party rallies as the girl who had done so well for the nation. She was as much an arm of state policy as the soldiers'.

Of course, said Dr. Mader, ordinary people are not supposed to know anything about this life of privilege. 'Athletes are as carefully shielded as missiles. Their families are given better jobs and bigger flats in return for handing their children over to the state. Ender's father was made a full colonel in the army after Montreal. I wonder if that had anything to do with his daughter's Olympic performances?' said Dr. Mader.

Life for the coaches and doctors was just as intense, he said. Their only thought was to 'get their man to win'. He continued: 'Anything that stopped an athlete doing well was blamed on us.

One swimmer had toothache on the way to an event. The dentist was told he was a failure and a black mark was put on his record. You didn't do that sort of thing twice. Our job was to make sure that the athlete competed and did as well as we knew he could. That was our only object. It had nothing to do with fair play or sportsmanship'.

There was no question of athletes having a bad day. 'We told them what they were capable of and how fast they should go. It was as simple as that. Sometimes when the club was doing badly we used to have public self examination sessions. We had to discuss our faults. The inquests went on and on . . . why, why did we go wrong? The orders kept coming down from Berlin telling us what we had to do'.

The future for Western athletes pitting themselves against this system, said Dr. Mader, is bleak; a view confirmed by the ever tighter stranglehold of the Communist states on important sports titles.

Planning for the Moscow games began before Montreal had finished. 'The motto for Munich was that Munich belonged to the West Germans but the medals belonged to us'. In Montreal we wanted to draw level with the Americans. For Moscow the motto is 'Bury the Americans and the West!' None of the Western

It is hard to believe, but Ilie Nastase is still technically a serving soldier in the Rumanian army.

nations will get a look in. The Communists have already agreed not to waste resources trying to beat each other in sports where they're already strong. The East Germans are concentrating on women's athletics, swimming, rowing and the Russians are concentrating on events like cycling and weightlifting.

When East German sprinter Renate Neufeld and her Bulgarian fiance Pensko Spassov defected to West Germany in 1977 the East German security forces were confident that she would not embarrass her former masters. Neufeld, they told the politicians, would have the common sense not to endanger her family with disclosures to newspapers. But the East German system is not noted for its flexibility and the wheels of retribution were already grinding into motion. Despite warnings from the security services that it would be better to leave the Neufeld family alone her father was dismissed from his job as an English language teacher in Berlin and her younger sister, a promising handball player, was dropped by her sports club. A few weeks later Neufeld, who said that she had stayed silent to protect her family, gave a series of lengthy interviews to West German newspapers and news agencies. Several years later her statement remains one of the most vivid and revealing accounts ever given by a leading Communist athlete.

Renate began serious training when she was five years old with a local sports club – the BSG factory sports society in North East Berlin. Three years later she was transferred to SC Dinamo in the Pankov district of the city; a club used to feed the high achievement clubs with young talent. 'To maintain our interest they used to offer prizes to the best. I remember that they would give us teddy bears,' she said. By the time she was nine Renate was running in her first Spartakiad: 'But you could only take part if you had achieved certain rankings'. In 1973, aged 15, Renate did so well in the national Spartakiad that the East Berlin 'Sports Echo' newspaper named her as one of the 'children of the Olympiad'. The newspaper wrote: 'This is a name we shall hear more of. You can be sure of that'.

By this stage talent alone wasn't enough. 'You had to have good knowledge. You had to know about Marx and Engels and industrial methods. We had to write essays on things like 'The leading role of the Soviet Union in the socialist camp'.

Her performances in the Spartakiad led to her being accepted by the KJS (Kinderundjugend Sport or children's and youth's sport school) attached to the elite club SC Dinamo Berlin. 'I was told that I was too small to be a sprinter. They said that I would have to be a

middle distance runner. But I dropped out of the first race. I didn't want to do middle distance. You get burnt out too quickly,' she said. Renate was marked down as a troublemaker and have to leave the school. 'Young people who don't do what they are told are avoided by the trainers'.

She returned to ordinary school and began training alone. During an exchange visit with a Moscow school she met a young Russian girl called Lena. 'I wrote to her when I got home and asked her to come and stay with me in Berlin,' said Renate. 'The secret police came round to see me and asked me why I had written to this Russian girl'. Lena came under pressure too. 'She wrote back saying that she didn't think the Berlin climate would agree with her'. Renate, it seemed, was still being considered for elite training, despite her row with the KJS, and the security police were anxious to prevent casual contacts with foreigners – even communist foreigners.

Bored with training alone and anxious for a chance to prove that she could develop into an international class sprinter, Renate wrote to the central sports authorities. 'They started checking my parents and grandparents. They found out that my grandmother lived on a private income in West Germany and asked me about that. They asked me if my parents had taught me good socialist principles. They asked me if I was a good Communist like Renate Stecher (100 and 200 metres champion at Munich)'. After three months intensive checking by the security services Renate was accepted by the KJS Ernst Gruber – attached to the TSC Berlin Club.

By now Renate had reached the fringes of the national team. 'All the athletes had to go to the central camp at Kienbaum. We had to call out our goals. It was a ritual. We were told that there were to be no friendship photos that could be misused. We were told to look aside if we met a West German,' she said. One girl, who had gone to Athens for the European Junion Championships, showed her photographs to the other athletes. It was, said Renate, done to motivate them, to tempt them with the prospect of foreign travel. But the girl was watched more closely than ever having been 'tainted' by travel to the West. Most of the trainers didn't have to worry about being corrupted. They, said Renate, were rarely allowed to travel abroad with the team.

Life centred around training, eating and sleeping. There was little else. 'We weren't allowed to watch Western television or listen to Western radio. That meant we were less informed than people outside. There was constant self analysis and evaluation. We had to write reports on each other and social behavior of our parents. We had to set tasks like collecting signatures against Chile or raising money for the American radical Angela Davis. By the end of the day we were dead. The Berliners amongst us were allowed out at weekends but the people from other parts of East Germany had to get special permission and had to justify their trip.'

Meals were carefully planned. 'The light athletes like me, the runners and jumpers, had one piece of meat. The heavy ones who threw the shot or lifted weights had three pieces and lots of sweets. We all felt sorry for the little girl gymnasts. All they got was crispbread and apples. There was always food around and we used to send it home. Some young boxers once swopped some oranges for some clothes. But they weren't punished for that. You see there aren't enough boxers in East Germany . . .' For special achievements, said Renate, athletes were given special privileges. 'We all heard that the ice skater Gabby Seyfert had been given a house.'

In 1976 Renate was handed what her trainer described as vitamin pills. The pills, as everyone knew, were in fact anabolic steroids, used by trainers to build up muscle and endurances in athletes despite the risk of infertility and liver tumours in women and heart disease and liver damage in men. In 1977 Renate, having refused to take the pills and under severe pressure to explain her actions to the security services, fled to the West. She now lives in West Germany with her Bulgarian husband Pentsko Spassov and their young son. Renate still runs, she says, but 'just for fun.'

'I had to sign a form promising absolute silence even to my parents,' she said. Her trainer Gunther Klann, constantly worried that his athletes would give away the details of training or privileges told her: 'If you have a boy bring him to us so that we can talk to him.'

From then until she defected Renate's life was determined by the master plan of the central computers described by Dr. Mader earlier. 'We had to do everything according to the plan. Even massage was done according to the plan. Every year we were examined and our potential was worked out. The doctors used to take blood samples from our ears and all the results were fed into the Computer. At the beginning of the season they would give us our perspectives – that meant we knew what we had to achieve.' In 1977 she was told that by the end of the season we would be running 24.45 seconds for the 200 metres. In fact she ran 24.27 seconds. Athletes who failed to reach their targets were summarily dealt with. 'One boy failed to satisfy them and had to leave. He became a waiter. He lost his perspectives. If you reach the perspective but aren't any good at academic work it doesn't matter. The official policy is that good sportsmen don't get bad marks. The teachers suffer if athletes fail in class.'

7 Drugs

Professor Arnold Beckett would have been happy to show us around the drug testing and research centre at Chelsea College, London, just a few yards from the famous King's Road. Unfortunately, the small, dark basement room, a jumble of mysterious looking tubes and gadgets, was locked for the day. He pointed to the dials by the heavy-duty door. 'It's a time clock and I'm afraid that I don't have the combination for today'. Why, we asked innocently, was it necessary to take such elaborate security precautions? He smiled: 'Ah well . . . you see this sort of thing is, well, still rather sensitive'.

Professor Beckett is head of Chelsea College's Pharmacy Department. He also happens to be a key member of the IOC's medical commission and the head of the British drug study centre, the only permanent centre of its kind in the world. This makes him one of the world's leading authorities on the use of stimulants, anabolic steroids and hormones in sport. Not surprisingly, the professor is rather unpopular in some quarters, especially behind the Iron Curtain. 'Oh no, the Communists don't like me very much. But I think they respect me. Put it like this – if I say something then they usually accept it'.

Back in his office, lined with sports photographs and medical tomes, he admitted that he was a worried man. Yes, there had been great progress since the commission was set up in 1967. But no, the battle had not been won. 'The Communists will do anything so long as they think they won't be caught. They don't mind breaking the rules. I am sorry to say that we are not in control of the problem yet'. Some sports experts go even further in assessing the threat posed by drugs. 'We are fighting for health and honesty in sport,' said Arthur Gold, the British President of the European Athletic Association and a vigorous crusader against drug abuse in sport. Lord Killanin, the Irish President of the IOC, said the problem was causing him to lose sleep. 'No sooner do the medical teams discover new ways to detect drugs like anabolic steroids than we hear of new drug problems, like the delaying of puberty in talented girl gymnasts. Everyone must be warned that the creation of artificial man is going to kill sport as we know it. The IOC's medical commission is doing its best but we must have the full backing of the world's sports federations to stamp out the evil. We need a change of attitude'.

Of course, doping in sport is not a phenomena of the 1970s. The Greek writer Milo of Croton noted that some unscrupulous athletes consumed massive quantities of goat meat before competitions to give them that extra something. In 1965 canal swimmers in Amsterdam used stimulants and fourteen years later French cyclists in a six day race were reliably reported to have taken cocaine, heroin, ether and caffeine. The first athlete to die as a result of taking drugs was an Englishman named Linton, who collapsed during the Bordeaux – Paris bicycle race, in 1886. During the early 1900s the situation continued to deteriorate. In 1910 a Russian scientist working for the Austrian Jockey Club discovered alkaloids in the saliva of some horses. By the late 1930s the practice had become common enough for lexicographers to include a new word in their dictionaries: doping, the use of narcotics, especially in sport. Meanwhile, the drugs industry was becoming more and more resourceful and athletes were eager to experiment with the new products. At the Winter Olympics in Oslo in 1952 officials were speechless when they saw the empty syringes scattered around the athletes' changing rooms.

The first doping 'sensation' came at the 1960 Rome Olympics when the Danish cyclist Knut Jensen collapsed and died. Doctors said that he had probably taken the stimulant Ronicol, which acts by opening the body's blood vessels. He was unlucky, said the doctors, because he had been racing in extreme heat and his body was already stretched to the limit. But it took the death of another cyclist, the Briton Tommy Simpson, to alert the world to the growing menace of drugs in sport. Simpson, probably one of the greatest ever racing cyclists, had always been reluctant to use drugs. 'I am riding up there with the stars and then I see their hands go up to their mouths and suddenly they are going away from me. I don't want to take dope – I have too much respect for my body – but . . .' he told a friend. Simpson succumbed to the temptation – and paid the ultimate penalty. He died on the slopes of Mount Ventoux during the 1967 Tour de France; doctors said from a combination of heat, alcohol and drugs.

As the sports authorities procrastinated the athletes got on with the business of taking dope. 'For the eight years prior to 1972 I would have to refer to myself as a hooked athlete. Like all competitors I was using anabolic steroids as an integral part of my training,' said the American Harold Connolly and a former Olympic hammer throw champion. 'Just prior to the 1964 Tokyo Olympics it seemed that more and more athletes were using steroids for athletic preparation and one began to feel that one was placing oneself at a decided disadvantage if one didn't get in on the sports medicine bandwagon. At the 1968 Olympics I knew any number of athletes who had so much scar tissue and puncture holes on their backsides that it was difficult to find a spot to give them a fresh shot. I'm saying this to emphasise my contention that the over-whelming majority of track and field athletes I know would take anything and do anything, short of killing themselves, to improve their performance.'

In 1963 a panel of experts working for the Council of Europe had tried to nudge the sports bodies into action by providing this neat definition of doping: 'It is defined as the use of substances in any form alien to the body . . . of healthy persons with the exclusive aim of attaining an artificial and unfair increase in performance in competitions . . .' When the IOC finally set up the medical commission four years later to stamp out drug abuse in sport it settled for a more cautious approach. 'We had the problems of deciding where to draw the line. How do you define the misuse of drugs? We didn't want to get into moral areas. We had to be pragmatic, to draw a line that we could hold,' said Professor Beckett. Instead of banning any substance that might improve an athlete's performance the commission instead banned drugs that might harm the athlete himself.

Even this modest objective – to stop athletes killing themselves – proved difficult to achieve. Did the IOC ban hay fever, headache or asthma pills just because they contained stimulants? Did they stop women athletes taking hormone pills to shift awkward periods? 'We wanted to be fair. We wanted to protect the athletes and indirectly to stop unfair competition' said the Professor. By the summer of 1979 the IOC seemed confident that they had resolved the tricky problems of definition. Stimulants, which had killed Jensen and Simpson, were apparently no longer a major threat.

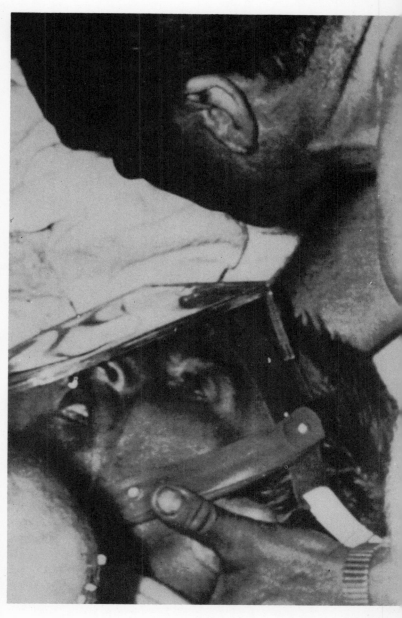

Britain's champion cyclist Tommy Simpson died from heat stroke aggravated by his drug-taking during 1967 Tour de France classic.

'There was no medical justification for taking many of them,' said the Professor Beckett. 'They give athletes a lift and reduce tension but they also can lead to aggression and loss of judgement. In some events, like cycling, this can be very dangerous.' One class of drugs – sympathomimetic amines like ephedrine – did pose a problem as they were often used in cold or allergy cures. The IOC found a way round this by saying that any athlete with an illness that might involve taking these drugs should refer to them. 'There are drugs available now to treat these illnesses which have no effect on the central nervous system. If we hadn't done that then we would have had excuses for taking these drugs.' There were no difficulties, however, in banning the narcotic analgesics, like heroin or morphine, as no athlete could possibly need to take them. Finally, the Commission decided that tranquillisers, sometimes used in events like pistol shooting where absolute calm is necessary, would have to stay off the list of banned drugs. 'They don't improve performance in most events and a lot of athletes use them to help them adjust when they travel abroad,' said the Professor.

The anabolic steroids, though, remain a worry. First developed in the fifties and in wide use by the sixties, both in the West and behind the Iron Curtain, they are, to quote Professor Beckett, 'synthetic chemical modifications of the male hormone testosterone in which the anabolic of muscle building actions are enhanced and the maleness actions of the hormones are decreased.' In other words, athletes who take them become heavier, bigger and stronger without, in theory at least, suffering radical sexual changes. The anabolic steroids can be used in varying doses by men as well as women, by sprinters and long jumpers as well as discus throwers or shot putters.

'I am very worried about these drugs,' Professor Beckett told us. 'The people who make them have tried to reduce the masculinity effects but it hasn't been possible to do that completely. Athletes who take them show greater competitiveness, aggression and drive. Large doses can, we think, lead to liver damage, fluid retention, personality changes, gastric ulcers and infertility. Some doctors also believe that they cause cancer. No doubt Swedish discus thrower Ricky Bruch would endorse the Professor's warning. In 1978 he told BBC television viewers that he had suffered horribly after taking anabolic steroids. Bruch, an Olympic bronze medal winner, listed side effects as: liver damage, a 100 lb gain in weight, mental illness, and so much general physical distortion that his Mother could scarcely recognise him. He had needed six operations as his body collapsed under its unfamiliar weight load. Finally he said he had just left hospital after an operation for a broken vertebra. 'I was one of those who started this terrible thing – I want to help stop it,' he explained. He said that other anabolic steroid takers had fared even worse, like the Russian whose testicles had exploded.

Although the IOC had first wanted to ban the steroids as early as 1967 they were not included in the official drugs blacklist until April 1975. Professor Beckett explained that it had proved extremely difficult to devise foolproof tests – 'Testing for anabolic steroids is not easy. It's expensive and requires well equipped laboratories and skilled staff.' However, by 1975 the crisis had passed in the West. Coaches and athletes now knew the terrible dangers of tak-

...zhova of Russia ...ning the women's ...t at Munich.

Above:
How women have changed: Orsolianov Capiva, a Russian javelin-thrower at the Rome Olympics, contrasts sharply with the drug-developed field sportswomen of just a few years later.

Left:
Parade of Soviet weightlifting champs, with super-heavy world record-holder Leonid Zhabotinsky at extreme right.

Right:
Juantorena of Cuba undergoing a dope test immediately after winning the 800 m in a world record time at Montreal.

ing anabolic steroids and by the 1976 Montreal Olympics, the first Olympics where testing for steroids took place, most Western athletes had got off the 'anabolic bandwagon'. There is no evidence that the Communists have followed this example.

Anabolic steroids can be taken until two or three weeks before a competition and still not be detected. 'They take athletes off the steroids and we can't prove anything positively when we test them at competitions. I certainly don't think the Communists are using them less. Did you know, for example, that you can buy these drugs over the counter in some eastern European countries?' said the Professor. In the late seventies the Communists managed to find a way to minimise the shock to an athlete who had 'come off' steroids. 'They are now injecting natural male hormones so that there is no rapid fall off in performance. These substances have a similar effect to the anabolics. They increase body weight and raise the ability of the body to perform tasks,' Professor Beckett said. the only solution, he added would be all round the year testing. 'If we could do that we would know who was using steroids. And we would be able to establish male hormone norms for athletes. Are we liable to get this sort of testing? Well, that's really a political problem isn't it?'

The East Germans are generally acknowledged as the drug masterminds of the Communist world. Professor Beckett, who has to work alongside the Communists on sports committees and at competitions, was understandably reluctant to discuss the allegation, made by one leading British sportswriter, that the East Germans were the 'biggest liars in

world sport'. Another sports scientist, who [wished] he wanted to remain anonymous, agreed [with] the claim. 'They are very good. Almost as ski[lful] technically as Western scientists. The Russi[ans] are not nearly as proficient. I believe that [the] East Germans provide much of the techn[ical] know-how for other Communists. [The] Bulgarians, who have had a bad doping reco[rd] rely heavily on the advice of the East Germa[ns].

It would be naive to suggest that tighter d[rug] controls at major sports events like [the] Olympics have not had any impact on the Co[m]munists. 'I think they are more cautious ab[out] using anabolic steroids,' said the Western sci[en]tist. 'The Russians say that they have introduc[ed] drug testing at domestic meetings but [one] shouldn't take this too seriously. One wonder[s if] this was done just to make sure that no trace[s of] anabolic steroids remained in athletes blo[od] rather than to see whether the athletes [had] taken the drugs'. Another scientist said that [the] Prague European championships in the autu[mn] of 1978 had illustrated this perfectly. 'The R[us]sians thought that the Czechs would be doing the testing for steriods. They didn't know that [the] West Germans were bringing their own equip[ment], which is far better and more effective th[an] the Czech's. It was quite amusing to see th[eir] faces when they saw what had happen[ed]. Shortly after the championships four Russia[ns] and one Bulgarian were disqualified for tak[ing] steroids.

The East Germans are more adept at avo[id]ing such embarrassing disqualifications. F[or] example, in 1978 they inexplicably dropp[ed] several of their most experienced 'heavy men' including the Olympic shot putt champion U[...]

yer and World Cup discus title holder
lfgang Schmidt – from the team which com-
ed at Crystal Palace, London. As Christopher
sher, one of Britain's most outspoken
rtswriters, pointed out: 'Neither was injured
he suspicious minds of Western journalists,
cials and athletes drew the conclusion that
East Germans did not want to submit some of
r athletes to dope tests . . .'

By the close of 1979 Western experts had built
a detailed picture of how the East German
ping machine functioned. Renate Neufeld, the
inter who defected to the West in 1977, said
t she had been forced to take anabolic
roids by coaches at the elite TSC Berlin club.
She was first approached by her trainer
ather Klann in 1976, a few weeks before her
birthday. He looked anxious, furtive and
d that he needed to speak to her in private.
asked if she remembered signing a pledge
er to discuss anything that happened at the
b. Yes, she replied, she recalled making the
mise. 'He handed me a bottle of pills. He told
that they were vitamin pills. According to my
ievement plan I was supposed to take the
lets two or three times a day and then stop for
days.'

Renate, who was on the fringe of full international honours, did as she was told. 'I noticed
that my legs began to get thicker and my voice
got huskier. I missed periods and a light mous-
tache started to grow on my upper lip. Some of
the older girls were having the same problems.
When I went for a massage the masseur said that
he could see I was taking the pills. 'In April 1977
Renate was selected for the East German 1980
Olympic squad. By then her leg muscles had
become so painful that she could barely walk.
Her voice would break and sometimes disap-
pear. 'I was worried that I wasn't a girl anymore.
The doctor at the club said that my thighs were
hurting because of cramp. He said my voice was
getting deeper because I had a cold. But I
decided that I wouldn't take any more pills. So I
hid them.'

It soon became clear to Klann that Renate was
no longer taking her 'vitamin pills'. He
demanded an explanation. 'He said that I had no
choice. I had to take them.' Still Renate would not
cooperate. A few weeks later she was dropped
from the team that travelled to Prague for a
match for what would have been her first sports
meeting abroad. Her monthly stipend was
stopped and she was accused by her coaches of

'not trying' and of 'not being a good Communist.' Klann said that she must be deranged if she suspected her trainers of lying to her about the pills. 'They told me to see the club pyschiatrist. But he was only there to try and influence us. I said that I wouldn't take the tablets.' The security services stepped in and asked why she was refusing 'proper medical treatment.' Soon after Renate Neufert fled to the West, taking with her samples of the pills. Later they were analysed by Professor Manfred Donike, of the West German Sports Federation, who described them as 'typical anabolica.'

The French newspaper *Le Monde* had, meanwhile, also compiled a dossier on the East German use of drugs. 'So as not to have an adverse effect on the athlete's self-confidence this medical doping is carried out without his knowledge, except in the case of 'safe elements.' Roland Mattes (100 and 200 metres backstroke champion at Munich) is said to be in this category and all the new techniques have been tried out on him . . . he is said to be the chief guinea pig. Treatment with anabolic steroids has been generalised, together with the introduction of male hormones for girls, even the very young. It is worrying to note the metamorphosis of the

young East German girl swimmers over the years. Once slim, slightly built and feminine, they soon become thick set and undergo deformations which indeed seem suspect. They inject swimmers with anti-fatigue vaccine . . . All these practices are freely tried out in swimming . . . Laboratories are at the disposal of the three chief trainers, fifty ordinary trainers and 120 doctors responsible for the development of swimming in East Germany . . . This is said to be the reason why no Westerner has ever been allowed into one of the special training camps,' said the newspaper.

Even when they are found guilty of taking anabolic steroids Communist athletes know that their careers are not over. At the worst they have to serve a two year ban. Sometimes they can return in time for the next important competition directly after the one from which they were disqualified. Ilona Slupianek, the East German shot putter banned after the European Cup final in 1977, was back in competition by 1978 when she took the gold medal at the European Championships in Prague. Arthur Gold, EAA President, signalled his disgust by walking out of the medal ceremony. Professor Beckett said that the present sentences were 'totally inadequate.' He said:

Russia's Nadia Tkacenke, world rec holder in the women pentathlon, was one five athletes banned life for failing anabol steroid tests during 1978 European championships.

A medical check-up f Vasily Alexeyev.

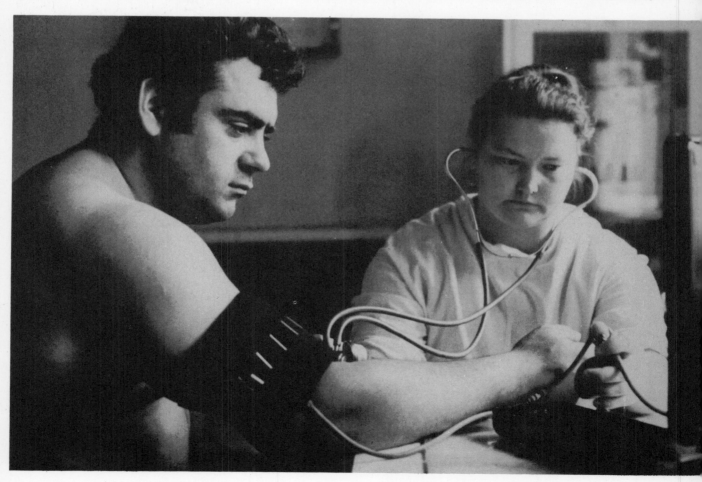

o years or 18 months just isn't long enough. It's culous that these athletes can come back so ckly.' Another sports official said after one A council meeting, in which the disqualifica- of a Russian athlete had been debated, that as 'absolutely sickening' to watch the East opeans support the Russians. 'They all came nd made political speeches supporting the sian representative. It was absolutely sick- ng'. The chances of any improvement seem . By 1979 Arthur Gold was under attack from East Europeans who wanted to remove him n his EAA position because, it was reported, is firm stand over drugs.

Western athletes, of course, are furious that ttle has been done to curb drug abuse by the mmunists. Geoff Capes, the British shot put- said that there was 'no point trying to com- e with countries ignoring the drug regula- s'. He said that it was time the 'Russians, East rmans and other Eastern Bloc athletes were ted out'. And he continued: 'They are not the t in the world. They just have the best doc- tors. They are laughing their heads off at the number of dope tests we have to go through in the West. There should be a group of experts who can go into these countries and test them at any time'.

What of the future? Professor Beckett remains pessimistic. It was unlikely, he said, that the Communists would find new, unknown drugs to pump into athletes. 'But they could find new uses for existing drugs. They could, for example, use anti-hormones to retard puberty in girl gymnasts'. They had also managed to work out ways of improving an athlete's performance without actually using drugs. Some doctors believe that if you change an athlete's blood before competing that will imrove performance. It's not illegal but it's certainly not ethical', he concluded: 'We have tried to draw the line. Ide- ally we would like to stop all drug taking. But we have to be pragmatic and we are just trying to hold the line we have drawn'. That is not proving easy.

8 The Future of Iron Curtain Sports

What thoughts flashed through Mark Spitz's mind as he mounted the rostrum in Munich to collect his seventh gold medal? While we make no claims to be mind-readers, the chances are that Spitz, the world's premier swimmer, was thinking about money. Olympic champions, even in their moment of personal and national triumph, have to make sober decisions: does it make sense, they ask themselves, to hang on to amateur status for another four years or should they 'cash in their chips'. In Spitz's case, cashing in the chips meant signing lucrative advertising contracts and launching a successful commercial career on the strength of his Olympic triumphs. Top-level amateur swimming, complete with the dedicated single-minded pursuit of gold medals, was no longer the supreme goal of the golden boy of US sport.

At the same swimming pool in Munich, the East German back-stroke specialist Roland Matthes winner of two golds, was having very different thoughts. For East Europeans, the Olympics are not a legitimate springboard into show business or the commercial world. Successful sportsmen are the servants of the state and the state insists that the bulk of the gold medal winners continue to contribute in some way to the nation's sporting and political achievements.

In a nutshell, these are the two competing philosophies of international sport. The commercial backdrop of all top-class sport in the West has led to the belief that sport should be apolitical. Money, and not the political requirement of the state apparatus is the determining factor. Scarce financial resources often place severe limits on talented Western teenagers who are trying to make the grade. But it is the political system, with its complex network of privileges and appeals to the Socialist sense of 'self-sacrifice' which is the crucial factor in sport behind the Iron Curtain.

These then are the two principal thorns in the flesh of the Olympic movement: on the one hand the over-commercialisation of Western sport which undermines true amateurism, and on the other hand the crushing political pressures on Communist athletes to perform well for the state. These are the factors which will decide the future course of the Olympic movement.

The original Olympic values have come increasingly under siege from both East and West over the past three decades. Let us look at the aims inherent in the founding philosophy of the Olympics as outlined by Baron Pierre de Coubertin at the end of the last century. There were four basic principles:

The principle of cultural achievement. The ancient Greeks believed that sport should be a cultural expression, a form of art which would arise out of natural competition. Coubertin thought that this belief should be revived.

the principle of human improvement through sport. Self discipline, competition, the recognition of betters, the constant drive to improve oneself: these were the character-building values which sport was supposed to teach. The Olympics, Coubertin believed, were to be the supreme goal for individuals of strong character.

The principle of fair competition. The strict enforcement of the rules by unbiased referees and the recognition of the authority of umpires was made a central tenet of the modern Olympic code.

The principle of armistice. Although many states are often opposed to each other politically when they enter the sporting arena, these differences should not affect the course of the Games.

These principles have been both undermined and extended ever since the Second World War. The extension of the original principles has generally worked to the benefit of sportsmen and women. the Games have, for example, been internationalised, since 1952. Instead of being confined to Europe and the US, the Games now include almost every Third World Country. Similarly the International Olympic Committee (IOC) has democratised the Games to an extent by banning discrimination on racial, religious or political grounds and by admitting women to the Olympics (although Coubertin specifically advised against this).

But the most significant development has been the relentless erosion of the four original principles by both East and West. As we have shown in this book, the principle of fair competition has long since been dropped overboard. There is simply no way of ensuring that everybody, has the same training opportunities and the same (or at least balanced) advantages at the start of a race. And, most significantly, the thrust of the IOC's campaign against doping is to ensure that there is 'no hazard to the individual's health' – that is, the committee is not primarily concerned that anabolic steroids or stimulating or retarding drugs, could give sportsmen an unfair advantage in competition.

It is clear from our conversation with Ea European sports officials that they no long regard the 'fair competition' proviso as in an way realistic. Body-building drugs are a integral part of the training course of every Ea European shot-putter. 'And why shouldn't we asked one East German official, who asked remain anonymous, 'the Olympics is about wi ning nowadays, not "playing the game".'

We have already demonstrated that th 'armistice principle' has also become an a acronism. Sometimes this is because of the vio ent, tragic intrusion of politics – the murder the Israeli athletes at the Munich Olympics, fo example – but more often because of the perva sive propaganda function of modern interna tional sport. Drugs and the robot-like educatio of potential athletes virtually from the cradle t middle age in Eastern Europe has also sabo taged the two remaining principles: that of ar through-sport and that of real character building.

So are these principles out of date? Should w re-think the Olympic ideal completely? O should we try to take the two subversive influ ences – commercialisation and politicisation out of international sport altogether?

One possible answer is to scale down th importance of the Olympics. There have bee proposals to return to a fixed-site Olympics probably based in Greece. This, some propo

Below right:
Olga Korbut retired from competitive gymnastics in Spring 1978. It is rumored that many of the current crop of girl gymnasts use drugs to inhibit puberty and physical development so that their bodies remain lithe and supple for as long as possible.

Below left:
Lyudmila Turishcheva is popular with youngsters eager to emulate the world champion's success.

altogether to watch Russian Valery Borzov in a vital Olympic race. The interest in the Olympics is quite unparalleled; by comparison the soccer World Cup, key ice hockey matches and the Spartakiad athletics meetings are like poor relations.

The way that the Soviets are determined to stick to the old model of the Olympics – which after all favours its system of 24-hours-a-day life-long system of training athletes – is demonstrated by its handling of the African boycott of the Montreal Games and the threatened boycott of the Mexico Olympics in 1968. South Africa was banned from the Tokyo Games in 1964 because of its refusal to abandon apartheid in South African sport. The ban had a shattering effect on the Pretoria Regime and it resolved not to let the situation recur. To this end, it promised to send a multi-racial team to Mexico in 1968 and it allowed a three-man commission from the IOC, led by Lord Killannin (now President of the IOC) to visit the country and inspect the progress in sports policies. While the commission expressed 'regret' about violations of human rights in South Africa, it decided that enough progress had been made to justify the readmittance of South Africa to the Games.

This was not enough to satisfy the Supreme Council for Sport in Africa (SCSA) composed of the national sports bodies of the black-ruled African countries which decided to boycott the

ents argue, would eliminate much of the financial strain – and attendant political controversy – which accompanies the construction of completely new facilities. The Montreal Games in 1976 was in the balance until only a few months before the start because of construction delays. A fixed-site Olympics would also mean that various countries would have to send smaller teams and that the propaganda effect would be somewhat dulled.

But would the Soviet Union and the US ever agree to this solution? The answer, certainly from Moscow, is an unambiguous 'no'. In East European society every sportsman is at least technically an amateur which means that the supreme testing ground will always be the Olympics. The US has incomparably more outlets for its blend of amateurs and professionals and this has tended to reduce the significance of the Olympics slightly over the past decade. For example, the US television audience for the world heavyweight boxing championship between Muhammad Ali and Joe Frazier, was as large as the audience for most of the Montreal Olympic events. In Eastern Europe, by contrast, factory sections sometimes stopped work

Games. There is evidence that the Soviet Union actually encouraged them to take this step and certainly within three weeks of the African announcement of a boycott, Moscow had declared that it was 'reconsidering' sending Soviet sportsmen to the Games. Many countries with pro-Soviet policies followed suit until over 40 countries had threatened a boycott of one sort or another.

Why did the Soviet Union threaten to boycott the Mexico Games? Sovietologists we talked to suggested that Moscow never had any real intention of sabotaging the Games – it had simply calculated that if it could command enough support it could pressure the IOC into changing its policies. There were two main reasons underpinning this: in the first place, the USSR was unhappy about its representation on the IOC which it thought was biased in favor of the United States and Western Europe. A direct challenge to the IOC would demonstrate to the body that Moscow's power did not end with the number of seats it had on the International Olympic Committee. Secondly, the Soviet Union wanted to show African countries – with which it was beginning to lose influence – that it would stick by its allies, even at the cost of not appearing at the Olympics.

It was a gamble which paid off. The IOC reversed its decision on South Africa which was banned from the Games again. The official explanation was based on the international climate' and the inability of the IOC to guarantee the safety of the South African athletes. The real reason of course was the IOC could not risk a head-on clash with the Soviet Bloc countries, especially when they were backed by the Third World.

Having established its power over the IOC, Moscow began to rein in its influence. It could not allow a similar risk to be taken again – the Olympics was too important for the Iron Curtain countries to play around with and, in any case, Russia was determined to secure the 1980 Olympics for Moscow.

This was the rationale behind the Soviet position on the African boycott of the Montreal Games. The boycott was not aimed specifically at the Pretoria Regime, but at New Zealand which maintained sporting links – through regular rugby tours for instance – with South Africa. Although the African countries were far from unanimous, about 20 countries, led by Tanzania decided to carry out the boycott. The IOC, concerned with the Taiwan issues did not react. The main reason that the IOC did not cave in as it had

Left:
Nadia Comaneci of Rumania, herself only 14, passing on the benefit of her experience to those that will follow in her footsteps.

Right:
Valeri Borzhov limbers up.

before the Mexico Games, was the *volte-face* of the Soviet Union. Several African delegates had approached Moscow and asked them to come out in favor of the boycott but the Soviet Union had undergone a remarkable change of heart since the Mexico Games. Politics, Soviet officials told the Africans rather glibly, should be kept out of sport. In fact, Moscow was simply concerned that the IOC would not respond to a boycott this year and that the USSR would be left out in the cold with the USA scooping all the important medals. Moreover there was the fear that the 1980 Olympics could be taken away from Moscow – and this was a move that the Russians wanted to avoid at all costs.

Fortunately for the Russians, perhaps, the Americans also have a vested interest in keeping the Olympics alive in its present form. That at any rate is the only conclusion to be drawn from the collapse of Western pressure groups' plans to boycott the Moscow Games as a protest against human rights violations in Eastern Europe. The Moscow Games are a particular watershed for the Iron Curtain countries. It is the first time in the history of the Olympics that a Games has been held in a Communist country – and it comes at a time when the Soviet Union is feeling particularly confident in its foreign policies. The Soviet grip on its East European

allies has not been seriously challenged since the 'Prague Spring' of 1968 which prompted the invasion of Czechoslovakia. And it seems to have won particular advantages in its relations with Washington, both in terms of real military balance and in letting the USA know the limits of its power. 1980 was a good year to hold the Games in Moscow. In the Kremlin's view – the demonstration of Soviet power and sporting prowess – would be all the more convincing.

The Western pressure groups – notably Jewish and Christian activists – had been pressing American President Jimmy Carter, himself a born-again Baptist, to announce a boycott of the Moscow Games. They argued that economic measures against the Soviet Union – trade sanctions or the banning of computer sales – were not enough to show US displeasure at Moscow's treatment of dissidents. The Soviet Union, they said, had invested so much finance and prestige in the Moscow Games that a threatened boycott by the US and the West would bring about a real change of policy. It was an overly optimistic – perhaps naive argument. But the human rights campaigners had certainly got one thing right: Moscow had invested billions of roubles in preparing for the Olympics and would fight hard to keep the Games if it came under boycott pressure from the West.

Left:
A lesson in a Ukrainian swimming school.

Right:
Net practice for an aspiring goalie at a special school for young soccer players near Leningrad.

The following short overview gives some idea of the scope of investment in the Games:

*Athletics – the Lenin Stadium, which seats over 100,000 spectators, has been renovated at a cost of 15 million pounds.

*Boxing/basketball – the largest ever covered sports hall in Europe has been built at a cost of 60 million pounds. During the Games it will be divided into two halls with facilities for 17,000 spectators at the boxing events and 16,000 spectators at the basketball.

*Swimming – linked to the boxing hall (situated on "Peace Prospekt" in North Moscow). A large, covered Olympia-pool is being built with separate units for swimming and diving. Water polo is to be played at a modernised pool in another sports complex.

*Volleyball – in a new hall built in the established Lushinski sports complex. Facilities for 3,000 spectators.

*Cycling – a new (cost at least 15 million pounds) indoor cycling circuit has been built and already existent tracks have been resurfaced.

*Archery – a new complex has been constructed to seat 3,000 spectators. Cost approaching 20 million pounds.

Gymnastics and Judo – substantial modernisation has been carried out on existing halls and spectator facilities have been extended. Estimated cost – up to forty million dollars.

Sailing – a new sailing center has been built in Tallinn in Estonia at a cost of thirty million dollars.

In addition there has been sweeping modernisation of football, handball, hockey and riding facilities.

The Olympic village has cost the Russians several hundred millions of dollars – though the buildings will later be used to house workers while the press center has cost fifty million dollars. On top of all this there is the cost of new hotels, new roads, of training staff, of setting up refreshment facilities.

Some of the construction work has been done with cheap or volunteer labor and we have heard reports (from ex-prisoner Nikolai Sharegin) that the Russian labor camps are engaged in making tourist knick-knacks for the Olympics.

But the fact remains that Moscow has ploughed a great deal of money into the Games and that a boycott would hit it hard. President Carter, however, has been reluctant, especially in the year of the Presidential elections, to antagonise relations with Moscow – and to irritate the many millions of Americans who are looking forward to watching the Games on television. A White House spokesman reported that the President 'did not think that a boycott would have the desired effect.'

The fact is then that both the Soviet Union and the West have a vested interest in preserving the Olympic games in their present form: as a mammoth large-spending political jamboree in which two opposing systems try to prove their point in a battle of strength. And sometimes produce some excellent sport.

Grace and beauty in the making at the Young Pioneer Palace, one of 8 specialist schools for budding gymnasts in Moscow.

But in the opinion of many experts something going to have to change if the Olympic movement is to survive until the year 2000. The general consensus is that the Olympic Games themselves will not change radically as long as the two super-powers are determined that the old system should survive. Of course, there may be some shifts – a democratisation of the International Olympic Committee is on the cards for instance. But the obvious conclusion is that something will have to change in the Soviet and American attitudes to sport before the Olympics can really get its house in order.

There are indications that the Kremlin is closely studying the progress of Cuban sport, for this could offer some useful lessons on how to run a sports machine at minimum cost and still produce results. Although the Soviet state allocation for sport is relatively small, the burden has fallen on factories, on the KGB and on the army. This has produced a fair number of sceptics within both the ruling Politburo and the military chiefs of staff. Is this expenditure really justified when the Soviet economy is going through an extremely difficult phase? These men point to Cuba, where on a budget of only about 120 million dollars, it is producing good results.

The main turning point will be the Moscow Olympics. If the Games prove to be a major propaganda triumph for the East Europeans, the doubters in the Kremlin will almost certainly be outvoted by the supporters of large-scale sports financing. This could have important and far-ranging consequences – if the Soviet Union is already so successful on limited funds, what will it be able to do with a bottomless purse? The structure of mass-and-elite sport will probably stay unchanged – but there will be massive injections of finance into drug research, an expansion of the training school systems (probably to include more potential athletes from the Central Asian regions as they are currently seriously under-represented in Soviet teams) and – as has been suggested by one British coach – there could also be a move to import coaching talent from abroad to improve the repertoire of certain sportsmen.

Whatever happens at the Moscow Games, Communist sport will soon have to make major decisions about its future directions. It will have to decide on the limits of co-operation with East European allies – notably East Germany – which are challenging its supremacy. It will have to clarify the role of sport in its foreign policy with the West – now that the Cold War is over, some Communist critics are suggesting that Russian sport could be used as a conciliatory device as well as a means of confrontation, as a sort of 'ping-pong diplomacy' with other states. It will have to decide too how much pressure it can continue to pile on its athletes and sportsmen – sooner or later they will reach breaking point and try to escape the rigid 'command and response' training patterns.

Communist sport has reached its most important crossroads. Its values have become outdated as those of the original Olympic charter. But Communist sports officials are afraid of experiments: they have a winning formula and they want to stick to it, minimising risk and squeezing as much out of their people and their system as possible.

Korbuts, Comanecis and Turishchevas of the future being groomed for their parts.

Below:
The sporting spirit can still cross frontiers.

127

Picture Credits

Photographs have been supplied by the following sources:

Popperfoto: Photographs on pages 8, 13, 15, 17, 18, 19, 20, 21, 22, 24, 25, 27, 30, 31, 32, 35, 36-37, 44, 45, 50, 54, 60, 64, 66, 68, 69, 70, 74, 78, 83, 85, 100, 103, 105, 109, 116, 123 and 124.

Colorsport: Photographs on pages 9, 10, 33, 34, 38, 42, 43, 47, 49, 53, 55, 56, 65, 70, 77, 86, 87, 91, 112, 115, 117 and 122.

Associated Press: Photographs on pages 12, 31, 33, 83, 85, 105 and 114.

Syndication International: Photographs on pages 21, 32, 45, 46, 48, 54, 58, 59, 63, 65, 72, 76, 95, 116 and 123.

Novosti Press Agency: Photographs on pages 6-7, 23, 27, 28, 40, 44, 49, 51, 52, 62, 63, 67, 72, 82, 84, 92, 93, 96, 101, 102-3, 106, 107, 110, 116, 118, 119, 120, 122, 124, 125 and 126.

Society for Cultural Relations with USSR: Photographs on pages 21, 22, 26, 29, 48, 73, 79, 80, 81, 82, 88, 97, 98, 104, 110-11 and 127.

Mansell Collection: The photograph on page 11.

Hulton Picture Library: The photograph on page 32.

The authors would like to thank the Daily Express for permission to reproduce the news article on page 61.